MEMOIRS
OF
A BABYLONIAN PRINCESS,
(MARIA THERESA ASMAR,)
DAUGHTER OF EMIR ABDALLAH ASMAR

VOLUME I

Elibron Classics
www.elibron.com

يا أيتها الاسم

Marie Thérèse Asm.

London. Published by Henry Colburn, Great Marlborough St. 1846

MEMOIRS

OF

A BABYLONIAN PRINCESS,

(MARIA THERESA ASMAR,)

DAUGHTER OF EMIR ABDALLAH ASMAR;

WRITTEN BY HERSELF,

AND TRANSLATED INTO ENGLISH.

Πότερον οὐχί πειρατήριόν ἐστιν ὁ βίος ἀνθρώπων ἐπὶ τῆς γῆς;

....

Les maux sont le marteau, la vie est une enclume;
L'homme, comme un métal, est né pour s'y forger,
Heureux, si cette épreuve a pu le corriger.

IN TWO VOLUMES.
VOL. I.

LONDON:
HENRY COLBURN, PUBLISHER,
GREAT MARLBOROUGH STREET.

1844.

PRINTED BY WILLIAM WILCOCKSON ROLLS BUILDINGS, FETTER LANE.

To Her Most Gracious Majesty,

THE QUEEN DOWAGER,

WHOSE NOBLE AND VIRTUOUS HEART IS EVER OPEN

TO THE AFFLICTED,

THIS WORK IS MOST HUMBLY

AND MOST RESPECTFULLY INSCRIBED,

BY HER MAJESTY'S

EVER GRATEFUL AND OBLIGED SERVANT,

THE AUTHOR.

PREFACE.

————•————

HAPPY are they who, during the early part of their days, have with a certain degree of smoothness gone through the trials of life, and in their mature age enjoy some peace and contentment! They can narrate at leisure, and with all the brightness of an untroubled mind, their past sorrows, the remembrance of which even adds to their present comfort. They may, indeed, fill with rich and elegant colours the chapters of their biography. But my case, gentle reader, is far from being similar, as will in the following pages appear clearly. Alas! how frequently did it occur, that while I was describing some past adversity or grief, much heavier calamities disturbed and oppressed my heart. Vain and unfaithful

world! Little did I suspect when, in my
father's house, splendour, abundance, and
every earthly comfort smiled around me, that
I should one day find myself isolated, abandoned, and destitute of every necessary of life!
Yet the merciful hand of Providence never
quitted me. Ah! without the unremitting help
of the Almighty, I feel assured, no woman's
heart or mind could have resisted the vicissi-
tudes and misfortunes that seared and withered
my existence!

Should I by this humble work succeed in
affording some new information to those who
take interest in the history of my country,
respecting the morals, manners, and private
customs of the East, and by relating the
events of my life, instruct the inexperienced
as to the advantages which may be taken of
incautious confidence, I shall consider myself
amply remunerated.

M. T. ASMAR.

London, May, 1844.

CONTENTS OF VOL. I.

CHAPTER IV.

CHAPTER V.

CHAPTER VI.

CHAPTER VII.

CHAPTER VIII.

MEMOIRS

OF A

BABYLONIAN PRINCESS.

CHAPTER I.

My Ancestors—My Parents leave Bagdad on account of the
Plague—My Birth in 1804, amidst the Ruins of Nineveh—
Residence at Bagdad.

I AM descended from a family in the East, who
derive their origin from the Brahmins, and have
long professed the Christian religion in the church
of Travancore; a church which, according to history,
was originally planted by Saint Thomas, the apostle
of our Lord in the Indies.   My ancestors, some
centuries ago, according to the tradition of our
family, left Travancore for Persia, and finally
migrated to Bagdad.   My grandfather, the Emir
Abdallah, was a man of great wealth, consisting of
lands and other property; including houses, silk-

works, sheep, and camels; of which latter alone he possessed five thousand.

Upon the death of my grandfather this great property descended to my father and his four brothers. It was my father's delight to employ all his influence, and a large portion of his riches, in plans for the propagation of the Christian faith. He himself professed the Chaldaic rite in communion with the church of Rome. His house was nevertheless at all times an asylum for the unfortunate of every denomination, whether Christian, Jew, or Mussulman. He built a house especially for the reception of strangers. He would go himself in quest of them, and, when he had found them, he would bring them in and wash their feet, and serve them at table with his own hands.

One individual, in particular, who sought an asylum in his house, when I was quite a child, I well remember. He was a missionary named Gabriel Dombo, who, for his zeal in the cause of religion, had been condemned to the cruel sentence of having his tongue cut out. This worthy man remained with us two years, and my father afterwards supplied him with sufficient funds to enable him to found a college for the instruction of missionaries.

The plague having broken out at Bagdad in the year 1804 with great malignity, my father found it necessary to retire with his family to a country residence which he possessed, amidst the ruins of Nineveh. It was called Kasr el Aza, which signifies the Palace of Delight. This was the period of my birth; which took place in a tent in the desert, a short distance from my father's house, whither my mother had retired to bewail the loss of several members of her family who had been carried off by the plague, as well as that of a beloved brother, who had come to his death by the bite of a serpent received while he was hunting, having first undergone the torture inflicted by a method of cure which has prevailed from the highest antiquity in Mesopotamia. Under this system the patient is prevented from sleeping, for five days, by the beating of drums, and by being pricked with needles, should he show any symptoms of drowsiness. During the whole of this time he is fed entirely on milk, with which he is constantly supplied until it causes him to vomit, when both milk and venom are supposed to be ejected simultaneously from the stomach.

To this torture was my unfortunate uncle sub-

jected during five days, but to no purpose, for the
poison had entered too deeply into his system to
be removed by any human means.

At length the plague ceased its ravages, but not
until, in its destroying course, it had swept away
entire families, and filled every house with mourning. My parents then returned to Bagdad, and
there I remained until I was four years old. We
resided at a spacious country mansion, distant
about an hour's ride from the city on the banks of
the Tigris, surrounded by gardens of vast extent,
abundantly stocked with date trees, sweet lemons,
and oranges, and fertilised by numerous streamlets
supplied from the neighbouring river. In this
delightful spot I passed the days of my infancy.
Many and many were the games of hide and seek,
which I played with my brothers, amongst their
numerous labyrinths; and the recollection of them
is, I think, at this moment, as fresh on my memory
as it was at any period of my existence.

Our next door neighbour was an Osmanli Aga,
a truly devout Moslem, noted for his scrupulous
observance of all the duties prescribed by the
Koran, and his horror of unbelievers, of whatever sect or nation. He detested a Shiàh with

as much cordiality as he did a downright Kafir. He never suffered a day to pass without repeating the due number of prayers, and going through the mattaniaths prescribed by the law.

I remember, when I was about eight years old, I was one day playing at hide and seek with my brother—at that age I was as nimble as a kitten; and, after an hour's play in the garden, the fancy took me to climb a large date tree, which was hard by the wall that separated our garden from that of this Mussulman. Here I secreted myself, enchanted with the idea of sending my brother on a fruitless chase after me all over the garden.

My trick succeeded to my utmost wish. Between the leaves of the trees I could see the little fellow running, first here and then there, and stopping at intervals to consider whether he had left any nook or corner unexplored; but never for a moment did he suspect the place of my concealment. After enjoying his embarrassment for a considerable length of time, I bethought me how I should make known to him the place of my concealment. At length, prompted, I suppose, by the genius of mischief, imitating as nearly as I could, the tone of the Mollah, who regularly summoned from the

nearest minaret all the true believers to prayer, I
cried with a loud voice—" La illahoun ila Allah
w' Mahommed rasul Allah."—" There is no God
but God, and Mahomet is his prophet." " El salat
akhsan min eltaäm."—" Prayer is better than food."
As it was just about the time of mid-day prayer,
my brother supposed it to be the voice of the
Mollah himself, until a loud laugh, which I could
not repress, at the success of my trick, discovered
me perched in my hiding-place. He was as much
diverted with it as myself; but when we returned
to the house, he was thoughtless enough to relate
the story of what had passed to my father.

Now my parent was as pious a Christian as ever
existed, and of so peaceable a disposition, that,
upon all occasions, he cautiously avoided giving
any offence, or offering the slightest insult to his
Mahommedan fellow subjects.   Instead, therefore,
of being amused at what I had done, he condemned me to a confinement for three days to my
own room, and gave directions that dates and water
should be my only sustenance, at the same time
impressing upon my youthful mind this caution—
" Knowest thou not that the very walls have ears?"

Over the garden wall of our Moslem neighbour

grew clusters of sweet lemons, of an enormous size. Days and days had I watched them, as they hung ripening in the sun, with a longing eye and a watering mouth, and many were the schemes which I revolved in my mind, to get possession of one of them. At length, like our first mother, whose sin is believed by many to have been committed at no great distance from this very spot, unable any longer to resist the promptings of the evil one, I became a perfect Bedouin. Several times I was foiled in my attempt by the unexpected appearance of my brothers or cousins. One day, however, when there appeared to be no danger of interruption, I directed a servant to place a ladder against the wall, and up I mounted. The forbidden fruit was now within my reach. With a heart beating high with hope and joy, but not unmixed with apprehension, I seized the largest lemon I could lay my hands upon, and descended the ladder with it. Whether the fruit derived its exquisite flavour from the manner in which I had obtained it, or whether it was in reality of superior excellence, I will not venture to decide; but I well remember that I relished it more than any

sweet lemon I had ever before eaten, and that I
have never since tasted one of equal flavour.

Here, however, my enjoyment ended. Like
other transgressors, I paid a heavy penalty for
the sin I had committed, in the remorse and
stingings of conscience which speedily followed it.
My father never omitted to read to his family and
household, once, at least, in the day, the ten commandments, and a portion of the holy scriptures.
Every day, therefore, when he came to the commandment which says, " Thou shalt not steal,"
my uneasy conscience smarted afresh. But not
content with merely reading the commandment, he
would frequently enlarge upon it, and pursue it
to its most remote application. " He who is faithful in small things," he would say, "is faithful
also in great : he who begins by pilfering trifles,
will become in time, by habit, a confirmed thief;
the only atonement is immediate restitution of
what has been stolen."

Unable, any longer, to support the load of remorse with which my mind became burthened by
this constant appeal to my conscience, I set seriously about thinking in what way I could make
reparation for the injury I had done our neigh-

bour; and as it was out of my power to return
the Moslem a lemon of so large a size as the one
I had purloined, I hit upon the notable expedient
of replacing it, by flinging over his wall three or
four of smaller dimensions.

With this expiatory act 1 concluded the affair
would have ended. Unfortunately, however, a
complaint was shortly afterwards made to my
father, that some member of his family had been
amusing himself by throwing fruit into his garden,
which had alighted on the heads of some of the
children who were playing in it. Upon this my
father immediately summoned all of us into his
presence, and subjected us to a rigid examination.
Of course, every one denied having any knowledge
of the circumstance, until it came to my turn to
be questioned. The maxims he had instilled into
me, which forbade the telling an untruth, even
though the object of telling it should be the salvation of the world, rushed into my mind, and I at
once made a full confession of what I had done.
I described the agony I every day endured while
at prayers, from remorse of conscience, and I
submitted myself to his will, expecting nothing
less than a long and severe penance. I was, how-

ever, most agreeably mistaken; for so high a value
did my parent set upon frankness and openness
of character, that he not only freely forgave me
for what I had done, but even went so far as to
chide my urchins of brothers, who had already
bestowed upon me the nick-name of "the lemon
stealer."

From that day to this I have never, knowingly,
said the thing which was not true. It was my
first trial; and the mastery which I then obtained
over the dread of consequences, has remained
with me, through good fortune and through bad ;
though, I am sorry to say, that my inopportune
ingenuousness has frequently made me commit,
what the French call, *bêtises*, and been the source
of much trouble. Whenever, in travelling in my
native country, I have had the misfortune to fall
in with a Bedouin, I never could help telling
him, not only that I had money about me, but
the actual amount of it. Had, however, the Wahabis, the Yezidis, and the other predatory bands
of Arabia, been the only beings to take advantage
of my failing, the consequence would have been
comparatively trifling ; but, alas, for civilization ! I
am grieved to say, that this weakness of mine, if

weakness it must be called, has been turned to far greater account in the most enlightened part of educated Europe, where the rays of knowledge are supposed to have dispelled the mists of our Asiatic darkness.

While I resided at Paris, a certain Duchess, whom I will not name, professed the strongest attachment to me. No term of endearment was sufficiently strong to express the intensity of her affection. Sister, daughter, I was every thing to her. She was a lady of shining talents, married to a man of considerable wealth, with whom, however, she had not lived for some time; but she possessed a handsome independent property of her own. During a long and severe illness, so incessant was she in her visits and attentions to me, that my gratitude knew no bounds. I think I could have laid down my very life to serve her. One day she called on me, and narrated a melancholy tale of pecuniary embarrassment. She told me of the large sums she had lost at the period of the French revolution, and concluded with soliciting a loan of four thousand francs. At hearing her request my heart leaped for joy. I could have embraced her for making it; so delighted

was I at the opportunity it afforded me of proving
the sincerity of my gratitude. My confidence was
blind. I considered the money as safe as if it had
continued in my own possession.

Not long after this, I received another visit from
my friend. After again going through a cata-
logue of her misfortunes, she hinted at a second
loan, and at last put the question to me point
blank. I was now compelled to tell her what was
really the fact, that I had no money at my dis-
posal; but, at the same time, with a frankness
perfectly Oriental, I said I had some valuable diamonds, which were entirely at her service. This
offer she eagerly accepted, and thanked me for
my kindness in a way which made the service I
had rendered her doubly pleasant to me.

As may have been anticipated, my dear friend
deceived me. In fact, she disposed of the jewels,
and threw away the proceeds at the gaming table.
Not content, however, with having despoiled me
of nearly all I possessed in the world, she was
unprincipled enough to solicit money, in my
name, of a Princess of my acquaintance, who had
shown me much kindness, pretending that I stood
in great need of it, and was too ill to call upon

her. By this artifice she alienated the affections of several of my best friends from me. She had frequently hinted to me her intention to leave me her property at her death, but, upon inquiry, it was discovered that it was so mortgaged over and over again, that she could not lay claim to a single para.

This is one of the many instances in which my misfortunes may be placed to the account of my confiding disposition. Yet, how could I suspect such turpitude in one whose conduct, up to that moment, had led me to consider her as a sincere friend? From early infancy the sacred injunction had been impressed upon my mind—"Judge not, that ye may not be judged!" I therefore looked upon it as highly criminal to think ill of any human being, and much more so of a cherished friend. Great indeed, therefore, was my astonishment, when at Rome, the Eternal city, the fountain-head of Christianity, I heard the maxim laid down—"Trust no one; though he should be thy own father." The facility with which I have so frequently fallen a victim to the artifices of design-ing individuals is doubtless to be laid to the ac-count of my defective education; I must, however, honestly confess, that in matters of this kind, I greatly prefer Asiatic artlessness to European cunning. The Bedouin of the desert always adheres to his promise; though in doing so he sometimes takes away your life.

It was some time before I could be persuaded that the duchess really intended to defraud me; but at length, when my eyes had been thoroughly opened to her perfidy, my friends advised me to institute a process for the recovery of the property. Nothing could be clearer than my case. The judge paid me a high compliment for my conduct in the transaction, and a decision was pronounced in my favour; but when I was expecting to reap the fruits of it, I had the mortification to find that the lady had made over the entire of her property to another, and had disappeared: so that I never recovered a single para.

To return to the days of my childhood. When a child I always preferred the society of my elders to that of those of my own age. I was never so happy as when in the company of my grandmother; an excellent woman, who lived to the age of one hundred and four years. Well do I remember the delight with which I heard the stories she related to me of her long and eventful life. I remember, too, with what breathless interest I listened to the wonderful stories my grandfather, who lived to a still greater age, would relate, of the events, which he had witnessed in the course of his long career. Never shall I forget with what feelings of horror I attended to his account of the siege of Mosul, by Nadir Shah, in the year 1743, which lasted many days. He used to tell how the Pasha, who governed the town at that time, and was favourably disposed towards his Christian subjects, issued his mandate, calling upon the inhabitants to supplicate God for deliverance, according to their respective modes of worship; and how the Christians thereupon, after the manner of the ancient Ninevites, essayed to turn away the wrath of the Almighty, by acts of charity, and deeds of mortification and penance, clothing their bodies in sackcloth, and putting ashes on their heads.

The town was defended with great bravery: for the inhabitants had determined to die rather than submit. Even the women and children exerted themselves with alacrity. Many assaults and breaches were made, but the assailants were constantly repulsed, and the breaches made in the day were repaired during the night. At length, the Shah, wearied by the obstinacy of the besieged, sent a peremptory message to the Pasha. stating, that he had succeeded in carrying a mine under the city wall, which he would straightway fire, unless the city surrendered. The Pasha refusing to capitulate, the mine was sprung, and a considerable portion of the town set on fire.

My grandfather lost several of his brothers in the course of this dreadful siege. He also lost a very valuable library, besides houses and other property, upon which he had expended a large sum. The Christians behaved upon this occasion with so much gallantry, as to gain the admiration of the Turks; and after Nadir Shah had found it necessary to raise the siege, and betake himself to Bagdad, some of the Christian churches having been greatly damaged, they were repaired at the expense of the government.

Of all our family I was my grandmother's chief favourite; so that when she died she bequeathed me her khelkhal, or anklets of silver gilt; her kirdan, or necklace, which was very splendid, having pendent strings of pearls and gold

chains all round; her kharanfel, or nose-jewels;
and her kamar, or girdle of jewelled gold; all
which proofs of her affection for me I kept with
religious care, until I was robbed of them in a public conveyance, together with many other valuables,
the gifts of my parents, to a considerable amount.

My mother had no fewer than eighteen children, of whom nine only survived, five boys and
four girls. I was the youngest daughter but one,
who died at the age of ten years. My other two
sisters both married. The younger of the two
was a girl of rare beauty. Her skin was delicate
and fair; her eyes were full and dark; and her
hair black, and as soft as the finest silk. Her form
was cast in the most perfect mould, and her whole
presence was full of dignity and grace. Neither
were her mental endowments inferior to those of
her person, though they had not had the advantage of European cultivation. Such is the true
portrait of my second sister, whose name was
Ferida, that is, "the incomparable." At the age
of twelve she was married to a wealthy sheikh of
sixteen, and at thirteen she had given birth to a
son.

This nephew of mine was the most preco-

cious little urchin I ever met with. Before he
was three years old he could repeat his paternoster,
and go through those compliments which, in eastern
countries, make the earliest part of education.
Before he was four he could read perfectly well.

My sister lived till she was thirty-five, and had
several children. But then, together with her
whole family, she was carried off by the plague.
In the space of a very few days there was not one
living soul remaining in that once happy family.
The seal of the Pacha, affixed to the door, to
prevent unholy pillage, announced the desolation
which reigned within.

CHAPTER II.

Heat at Bagdad—Domestic Manners of the Inhabitants—A
Journey to Persia—Rejected Treasures—Religious Studies—
Persecutions of my Family—I retire to a Convent.

FROM the age of four to eleven, my time was
spent partly at Bagdad and partly at Mosul; at
which latter place my family usually passed the
summer months, in order to avoid the excessive
heat which prevails in the once celebrated city of
the caliphs during that season. Such, indeed, is
its intensity, that the inhabitants are compelled to
spend the middle of the day, when the sun's rays
have their greatest influence, in the "serdab," a
subterranean apartment, built for the express purpose, which is kept comparatively cool by constantly sprinkling it with water, and by the action
of an immense fan, which rests on the ground, and

is moved backwards and forwards by slaves. Here
they remain till the evening, when they betake
themselves to the terrace or roof, to enjoy the
refreshing breezes.

During the hottest months, when the ther-
mometer is often at the height of 120° Fah-
renheit, the ladies wear a silken garment or
chemise, and "babouches" or slippers, but no
stockings. At night it is the custom to sleep
on the terrace, at the top of the house, in
the open air; the ladies, the men, the children,
and the domestics having each their separate
terraces. Strange as it may sound to European
ears, it is by no means an uncommon practice with
the ladies of Bagdad, in the months of July and
August, to steep their night clothes in cold water,
which is slung up for this purpose in skins, in
order to keep it as cool as possible. Having
done this, they put them on wringing wet, and
again retire to their beds of palm branches, to enjoy
refreshing slumbers. Notwithstanding this practice, rheumatism, so prevalent in England, is
rarely heard of in that country. In July, persons
whose occupations compel them to be abroad, are

in danger of suddenly being suffocated by the *samiri*.

The habit of early rising is universal at Bagdad. The sun never darts his morning ray on a closed pair of eyes; and every one, rich as well as poor, carries down from the roof his or her mattrass, which would otherwise be speedily burned up with the heat.

Bagdad is celebrated for its good cheer. The inhabitants make four meals in the course of the day; beginning at an early hour with coffee. This is followed by the "nerghila," or pipe. At nine a breakfast is served, consisting of a preparation of milk, thickened to the consistency of cream-cheese, rice milk, and dates cooked with butter. The hour of dinner is one; and prayers are first scrupulously performed before every meal.

The ladies of Bagdad wear a head-dress peculiar to themselves. It consists of a large black and white izar, or veil, manufactured at Mosul, of silk and cotton mixed, and descends from the head almost to the feet, somewhat resembling the Spanish mantilla, with a bandeau of horse-hair, which encircles the head, covering the face so as to conceal the features of the wearer, but, at the same time to allow, in the true Eastern fashion, the full exercise of her own curiosity. Out of doors, it is impossible to discover the rank of a lady from her costume, as they one and all, rich as well as poor, adopt the same sober, unpretending garment. Within doors, however, the case is widely different; for here the ladies of Bagdad exceed almost all the other women of Turkey in the costliness of their attire. Rich silks, ornaments of gold, pearls, and jewelry of high value, are worn with lavish profusion.

When I was eleven years old, my father took me with him on an excursion to Persia. We started from Bagdad to Shiraz; whence we travelled to Ispahan; in the neighbourhood of which city, I remember my father drew my attention to an emerald mine, the circumstances connected with which are somewhat curious. According to the account he gave me, it would seem that this mine was formerly exceedingly productive, and yielded an annual supply of the most beautiful jewels that the imagination can conceive. It so happened that the reigning Shah had at this time a serious quarrel with the Grand Seignior, which he was very anxious to terminate in the most amicable manner. After deliberating for a long while as to the mode most likely to affect this object, he bethought himself of sending a present of jewels from his renowned emerald mine.

Accordingly, he sent by the hands of his own vizier presents of an immense value, consisting of a massive gold tray, rough and bristling all over with emeralds, and twelve golden cups inlaid, each filled to the brim with the same precious stones. Besides these, there was a golden " lakan," or washing apparatus, so covered with them as to surpass the fields of spring in dazzling verdure.

Against such peace-offerings as these, " the centre of the universe " felt perfectly satisfied that no extreme of wrath, however deadly, not even the blind anger of a follower of Omar, could hold out. The Shah was nevertheless doomed to disappointment. By an unfortunate blunder, the Vizier he had selected as the bearer of these precious gifts happened to be known to the Sultan as a violent opponent to the interests of the Porte at

the Court of Persia. When, therefore, he appeared
at the feet of the Shah to present his peace-offer-
ing, the haughty potentate exclaimed, scornfully,
" What dirt is this you would have us eat? Go,"
he said, turning to one of his attendants, " and see
them carried to the least worthy part of our
palace." With a heavy heart, and bursting with
rage and mortification at the ill-success of his
mission, the Vizier set out on his way back; but
not without serious misgivings as to the length of
time during which his own head and body might
be permitted to enjoy each others society.

The "shadow of the Almighty on earth," who
could not for a moment entertain the idea that
such paltry considerations as the welfare of his
subjects, or the honour and dignity of his empire,
could have any weight in the scale against the
aforesaid gold and jewels, looked forward with
confidence to the success of his mission. On
learning the reception his Vizier had met with, his
anger knew no bounds. He swore by the holy
prophet, and by his own beard and head, that he
would be avenged. After exhausting the Persian
language, that fertile source of imprecation, he

gave strict orders that the mine, the source of his humiliation, should be closed for ever, as though a man should cut off his nose to prevent his enemy from pulling it.

One of the objects of my father's journey into Persia was, to make inquiries respecting this mine; as, amongst his projects for repairing his shattered fortune, that of re-opening and working it was one. He did not, however, live to carry the design into execution. From Ispahan we proceeded by way of Teheran to Mosul; whence I shortly after accompanied my father in an excursion through Mesopotamia, in various parts of which country he had considerable landed possessions.

On our return from this journey, I spent my time chiefly at Mosul, devoting myself almost entirely to religious studies and devout contemplation. In this way I passed three years of my life, without the occurrence of any event of sufficient importance to call for particular observation.

According to the custom of the East, where betrothals take place at a very early age, I had been engaged at my birth to a very young sheikh, a distant relation of the family, he being at that

period only three years and a half old. When
I was twelve, and he, of course, only fifteen
and a half, my father made preparations for the
marriage. But I had a strong desire to remain
single. From the age of six I had been in the
habit of reading the lives of the Fathers, and I
had formed a determination to follow their example. There had been many weddings in our
family, and the festivities on the occasion generally
lasted several days; yet I never participated in
them. On the contrary I betook myself to my
favourite books, the histories of saints, hermits,
and martyrs; and the more I read, the more
intense was my desire to share in their sufferings
and their glory. My father, indeed, had rather
encouraged me in the course I was pursuing;
and upon one occasion, when he accidentally
found me reading the Arabian Nights' Enter-
tainments, he reproved me severely, and confined me to my room for three days; during
which I was only allowed bread and water.
From my love of solitude, and retired habits,
I was called by my parents " Bechmel Biri,"
the daughter of the Desert; a name given to

the turtle-dove, which, according to Oriental tradition, when it has lost its young, flies to the
Desert, and sings itself to death.

With a presentiment of the career of suffering
to which I was destined, I made every effort in
my power to induce my father to break off my
intended espousal with the young sheikh, but in
vain. I thereupon addressed myself to the youth,
who, like myself, was under the influence of
strong religious impressions; and on express-
ing my determination to become a nun, he resolved to take the vows of a Trappist; to which
Order he attached himself, and now lives in a
hermitage on Mount Lebanon, at the foot of the
cedar mountain, on a ledge so precipitous, that a
bird would hardly dare to make her nest on it.
We parted with mutual regrets, and oft-repeated
hopes, that, though our religious duties compelled
us to separate on earth, we should, when our
earthly tribulations were over, be united in
Heaven.

I was particularly fond of riding, and often
accompanied my father and brother in their
excursions. We frequently wandered through

fields of corn, which grew to so great a height as
entirely to conceal us. One day we were riding
out, and had taken with us a beautiful young girl,
whom I loved with the affection of a sister. We
were about a three-hours' ride from Mosul, near
a little village called Karagossa, when about fifty
armed Arabs surrounded us. My father and
brother carried arms; but it would have been
madness to attempt any thing against a force
which could easily have destroyed us, or carried
us off prisoners. The chief of the Arabs did not,
however, offer us any violence; but, struck with
the singular loveliness of Mariam, for that was
the name of my friend, he insisted on carrying
her away with him. We earnestly expostulated,
but our entreaties were unavailing; and, with the
deepest anguish, I beheld the loved companion of
my youth torn from me by a band of lawless
robbers, who, quick as lightning, made off with
their prize. My brother lost no time in collecting
a force sufficiently strong to have re-captured her;
but the Arabs were well mounted, and the swiftness
of their steeds rendered it impossible to overtake
them.

Mariam had been passing some time with us, and it was intended that she should remain still longer. Her parents, therefore, were entirely ignorant of the peril into which their beloved daughter had fallen; and, as we trusted by active exertions to recover her, we wished to spare them the anguish which the knowledge of her misfortune would have occasioned them.

My father caused inquiry to be made in every direction, and succeeded at length in discovering the retreat of the Arabs; who engaged, upon the payment of a heavy ransom, to restore their prize to the arms of her distressed friends. The sum they demanded was fifty purses, or close upon six hundred pounds in English money. This my father most gladly engaged to pay; and, immediately afterwards, I had the happiness to see my beloved friend once more under our roof. She related to us that she had been treated by the Arabs with the utmost consideration, which had greatly diminished the horrors of her captivity. The chief, though ardent in pressing his suit, had offered her no violence; neither had he resorted to any threats, for the purpose of terrifying her into compliance. She declared that she could not avoid being touched by the generosity of his conduct throughout.

Both of us were enthusiastic for the cause of religion. I scarcely know on which side the greater zeal lay. Her personal charms were of a high order, and of that description which, at first sight, strikes the beholder of the other sex with admiration. But she heeded not their attentions, and had no desire to make conquests; her whole soul being absorbed in religious meditation, and nearly her whole time passed in pious observances. At midnight, we frequently rose and passed hours together in acts of devotion. During Lent our food consisted of vegetables, boiled with rice; of which we partook sparingly once a day. On Sundays we frequently walked into the fields, and, collecting around us a number of our own sex, we instructed them in the principles of our faith. Hundreds were sometimes attracted to the spot, where, seated on the grass, they would attentively listen to our discourses. Like myself,

Mariam had come to the determination to lead a life of celibacy, and to dedicate herself to the advancement of the true faith. This determination on our part caused us to be regarded with wonder, by all who knew us and were acquainted with our vows; for I was the first woman who, since the Mussulman dominion, had devoted herself solemnly to a life of celibacy in my neighbourhood, and my friend was the second.

At this period the Christian Church at Mosul enjoyed singular immunity from persecution, under the mild and tolerant rule of the Pasha at that time in power.

With the good Pasha's death things assumed a different aspect, for his successor was a stern and headlong fanatic; the sworn enemy of Christianity, he panted for an opportunity to wreak his vengeance on the heads of its followers.

The reigning Pasha, having gained intelligence of my proceedings, and being determined to strike a decisive blow to check the spread of what he regarded as pestilential doctrines, and, if so it might be, to uproot them utterly from the land of

Islam, appointed a day, on which all Christians
were commanded to repair to a certain spot, there
to renounce their faith, and publicly embrace that
of Mahomet.

Many rejoiced in the prospect of suffering for
Christ's sake, and looked forward to martyrdom
as a short and glorious passage to the mansion of
glory promised by the great Father of our faith
to those who should hold fast to the Rock of
Salvation even unto their life's end. My uncle,
who was Archbishop of Diarbekir, my father,
Mariam, and myself, were amongst this number.
In company with those, whom neither chains,
torture, nor death could tempt to deny their
God, we went in procession, chaunting hymns of
praise and triumph, and almost believing that we
saw the heavens opened, and beheld the crown
of martyrdom extended.

We were taken before the Pasha, who had threat-
ened to take our lives, and, I doubt not, would have
kept his word, had not the charms of my companion turned aside his fury.

On being arraigned by the Pasha, we boldly

entered upon the controversy, maintaining the
truth of our faith, and endeavouring to convince
him of his errors; but he was not a man of words,
nor did he care to assert, still less to prove, the
truth of his own faith. He threw us into prison.
As for my friend and myself, we were shut up
in a room of the Pasha's palace, but our unhappy
companions were straightway dragged to a dungeon, and received daily two hundred blows of the
bastinado.

I was sometimes allowed to visit them in their
dark and loathsome cell, and could not restrain my
tears on seeing my beloved parent and relations
loaded with heavy chains. They, however, were
not cast down, but, kissing their chains, exhorted
me not to weep, but rather to rejoice, that they
were accounted worthy to suffer for Christ's sake,
even as his disciples.

They were daily brought out into a court to
receive the bastinado, and I was forced to hear
the cries of my father, my brothers, and my
uncles (one of whom was branded on the forehead with hot irons,) without being able to

c 3

alleviate their sufferings, or even to speak a word
of comfort to them under their trials. One of my
uncles died under the torture. My father and
the rest of his relations were at length released,
upon paying enormous sums to the rapacious and
cruel tyrant who was the cause of their misfortunes.

The Pasha having enriched himself, and in some
measure sated his religious enthusiasm, by this fla-
grant outrage on my family, and wholesale plunder
of their property,—we were permitted to enjoy an
interval of repose, and to return to our former way
of life, without interference or molestation.

We resided at this time in the town of Alkoush,
about twelve hours distant from Mosul, near which
was situated a convent of considerable size. To
this retreat I obtained my father's permission to
retire, and a small room was prepared for me,
the furniture of which consisted of a bed, made of
the leaves of the palm tree, a small carpet, a skull,
and a crucifix, with a number of books, comprising
a copy of the Holy Scriptures, and the lives of
those holy men who had devoted themselves to

prayer and contemplation, among which was the life of St. Anthony of Egypt.

In this sacred asylum my days passed in quiet, if not in happiness. I rose at six, and remained on my knees for two hours engaged in prayer and meditation; then, taking my Bible, I read a certain number of chapters, after which I read for some time portions from the lives of the saints, and concluded by reciting fifty of the Psalms and other canticles, which occupied me till noon, at which hour I left my cell and wandered in the convent gardens, sometimes penetrating beyond them, and climbing the steep mountains which surrounded our dwelling.

As I ascended, magnificent views opened around me on every side, the Tigris was at my feet, and wild romantic scenery surrounded me in every direction. For hours would I remain rambling over these lofty hills, my thoughts employed in the contemplation of nature, thence ascending to the divine author of all things, till songs of praise would break from my lips.

At four o'clock I usually returned to take a light and simple meal, which consisted of bread and

fruit. Every Sunday my parents supplied me
with these necessaries. A servant was charged to
bring me weekly a large loaf, and enough dried
fruits to last till the following Sunday.

CHAPTER III.

Removal to Alkoush—Design for elevating the Female Cha-
racter, and establishment of Female School—Visit from the
Sister of the Pasha of Mosul—Ramazan—Visit to the Pasha's
Harem—Flattering Reception and Hospitable Treatment—
Dinner—The Amira's Parrot a True believer—Return Home.

SIX months had passed over my head since I
first entered the convent, at the expiration of
which my father, brother, and two of my uncles
set out for Bagdad, while my mother, with the
rest of her family, went to reside a mile or two
from Mosul, amid the ruins of Nineveh, in a small
village the greater part of which belonged to my
father. My mother would not hear of leaving me
behind. I therefore accompanied her, and, finding
at a short distance from our habitation the remains
of a deserted convent, I took up my abode there,

passing my time, as before, in prayer, meditation, and fasting. Some portion of every day
I devoted to literary pursuits, and composed
several books on religious subjects. After some
months residence in this secluded habitation, I
formed the determination of founding an establishment of learned women, and prevailed upon two
friends, one from Mesopotamia and the other from
Persia, to join me in my retreat.

The inequality of the sexes had long been to me
a subject of indignation. I saw Christian women
treated almost like slaves, their understanding uncultivated and left in the grossest ignorance, while
men enjoyed every advantage of education. I.
therefore, determined to do all in my power to
educate those of my own sex. One of my cousins
undertook to give lessons in Kurdish, Chaldee,
and Turkish; and I had a friend, a lady of great
intelligence, who taught the Persian language.
Numbers were attracted to our institution, in
which no branch of education was neglected, and
we were joined by many ladies of rank.

During this period I did not neglect the poorer
classes, but constantly preached to them in the

open air, giving them lessons of prudence and piety; thus labouring, as I hoped, not only for their good, but for that of generations to come. A shepherd of my father's, a Bedouin by birth, together with his whole family, was persuaded to embrace the Christian faith.

Whilst I was an inmate of the convent, I was visited by many ladies of consideration from the neighbourhood, and, amongst others, by the sister of the Pasha, a woman of some learning, but, nevertheless, a great fanatic.

Her visits to me were necessarily secret, for so violent is the fanaticism, so bitter and intolerant the public prejudice against those professing the Christian faith in those parts, that not even a person of her exalted station could venture to pay an open visit to one so identified with the obnoxious creed as myself. Instead of being accompanied, therefore, by forty or fifty slaves, the ordinary retinue of a lady of her rank, she was never attended in her visits to me by more than four, two of whom were male and two female.

Our conversation turned on religion, for, being,

as I have already observed, a woman with some
pretensions to learning, and animated by a zeal
for the acquisition of knowledge, she was extremely curious to learn the principles of the
creed I professed, and which appeared to have
produced so marked and so enduring an effect
on my conduct and habits of life. In order to
assist her in this I gave her a New Testament,
which she took great delight in studying.

On one occasion, during a conversation which
lasted three hours, I made a strenuous effort to
lead her from darkness to the true faith. I expa-
tiated largely and fearlessly on the glorious truths
of the Christian religion; I used every argument
which my reading could supply; I omitted no
means of proof, nor failed to avail myself of any
analogy which my fancy could suggest, for the
purpose of convincing her of the superiority of the
Christian faith over all other creeds, the offspring,
as I laboured to convince her, of human error and
invention.

I did not fail to point out to her how these
impositions had been fastened upon the minds of
their credulous and ignorant brethren,—who, from

the absence of all education and moral enlighten-
ment, were absolutely the prey of any delusion,
however absurd, to which they were incapable,
alike from ignorance and indifference, of offering
any resistance,—by ambitious adventurers, soli-
citous only for their own advancement, and either
instigated by hatred towards their fellow-men, or
animated by the lust of conquest and the thirst for
fame.

God, the only true God, the everlasting Father,
the Creator of the universe, the Giver of life, was,
I told her, the Author of the Christian religion,
and, in proof of my assertion, I referred her to the
Bible, which I knew she was much in the habit
of studying, and for which she entertained great
respect.   I also proved to her that Mahomet
himself had borrowed his Koran mostly from
the sacred volume—a tribute to, if not a proof
of, its truth.

These, and other arguments of a similar kind,
which, I hoped, might tend to her conversion, did
I unweariedly urge during our long interview.
The princess was astounded.   Such language had
cost many a Christian his head.   Had not her

brother, in the course of that very year, put
to death multitudes of Christians, who had dared
to avow their faith, and set at nought the established religion?

What, she asked me, could make me so far
regardless of my safety as recklessly to indulge
in language which, if carried elsewhere, might
cost me my life?

I replied that I had long earnestly desired to
suffer martyrdom in the cause of the Christian religion, if such should be the will of God. " God,"
I exclaimed, " who does all for our good, and dis-
poses events according to his supreme will, will
not permit me to suffer, unless it seem good to
his Almighty wisdom."

At this display of resignation to the will
of Providence, so perfectly Mahomedan in its
character, the princess seemed surprised, and
began to show me greater respect than before,
struck by the exhibition, in a Christian, of a
virtue, occupying so high a place in the faith
which she herself professed.

After a mutual interchange of the customary
compliments, the princess returned to the Zenana,
in the same private manner as she had come.

Immediately after our interview ensued the fast of Ramazan, during which, as most of my readers are probably aware, the Turks attend to no business of any kind, fasting, with great scrupulousness, from sunrise to sunset, when, having first washed and perfumed themselves, they proceed to indemnify themselves for their past mortification by eating and drinking, in which occupation, interspersed with reading from the Koran, they pass the whole of the night, during which a general illumination usually prevails.

Our conversation seemed to have made no inconsiderable impression on my illustrious visitor; for, at the termination of Ramazan, she sent me an invitation to dine with her. She had already given me repeated invitations, but my friends, apprehensive for my safety during the continuance of the fast, would not permit me to accept them. I was myself far from desirous of paying this visit, for many reasons; one of which was the necessity of putting off my usual dress (that of a recluse) and appearing in a garb more suited to the guest of so distinguished a personage.

Whilst these considerations passed in my mind,

my conscience told me that my visit might, perhaps, be the means of reclaiming sinners, and diffusing the saving light of truth, where all before had been dark and without hope; and this admonition quickly putting to flight all personal considerations, and overcoming all personal apprehensions, at once determined me to go, if, peradventure, I might bring into the fold some of the lost sheep of Israel. I should have liked to have taken with me a young friend whom I greatly loved; but the invitation being strictly confined to myself, I did not dare to take any step which might put the Amira to inconvenience.

In a strictly private manner, attended only by two slaves, I set out for the Zenana, with a heart full of joy, elate with the hope of making converts to the true faith.

I was superbly dressed. My *ghombaz*, or dress, was of white gold tissue, open in front, after the manner of the east, with ample sleeves of the same material descending to the knees, and confined at the waist by a girdle richly embroidered in gold. My *sherwals*, or trowsers, were of crimson silk. Around my ankles were fastened anklets of silver gilt, richly chased, and babouches, or slippers, covered with gold embroidery, were on my feet. These, with a turban of white muslin embroidered with gold, and a Persian shawl thrown round my waist, completed the costume in which I went to pay my first visit to the Amira.

Alas! who would recognise in the forlorn and wretched being who now pens these lines the lively, gay, free-hearted, and enthusiastic creature of that hour—with a heart full of susceptibility and joyous frankness—breathing high with the hope of leading my wandering fellow-mortals into the way of truth?

When in the darkness of adversity, with failing faculties, I look back on that day, and think of the wreck which sorrow and bitter calamity have made me, my soul recoils with horror, and I sink into the abyss of sadness. Long suffering has weighed down my spirit and broken my heart; bitterness has become my portion, and my joy is turned to wailing. "For the enemy hath persecuted my soul; he hath brought my life down to the earth; he hath made me to dwell in darkness, as those that have been dead of old, and my spirit is in anguish within me ; my heart within me is troubled." But to return to my narrative.

On arriving at the door of the house, I was met by an old eunuch, who came to conduct me into the presence of the Princess. After passing through three or four doors, fastened with padlocks, of which he carried the keys, he led me into a spacious court, paved with marble brought from Diarbekir, which was polished to such a degree as to present the appearance, when viewed obliquely, of a huge horizontal mirror. It required, in fact, no small degree of dexterity to get safely across this court; for it was like walking upon ice. As I entered I observed three negresses, who had just been engaged in cleaning this polished pavement, and were gathering up their apparatus ready to depart.

In the midst was a superb marble fountain, with numerous jets d'eau, disposed with considerable taste, and on the left the Iwān, a chamber open the entire length of one of its sides to the court, from which it was only separated by a step The walls of the Iwān were decorated with a variety of ornamental arabesque devices, executed in different colours, mostly of a dazzling and marked kind. A splendid Persian carpet covered the floor; while the " takht," or large centre cushion, was covered with brilliant scarlet velvet, handsomely embroidered.

Through a door on the left of this chamber I was conducted into an immense saloon, which far surpassed, in the splendour of its decorations, the apartment I had just quitted. The carpet was of still more exquisite Persian manufacture, and the musnud was covered with red and green velvet, and embroidered in the most costly manner, the result of many a month's toil.

I had not had time to examine half the beauties of this saloon when the Pasha's sister made her appearance. Nothing could exceed the courtesy with which she received me. After the first formalities were over, she insisted on placing me by her side on the musnud, and absolutely overwhelmed me with compliments and civilities.

At this moment three Jairiahs, all beautiful young girls, principally from Georgia, Circassia, and Kurdistan, with skins of dazzling whiteness, radiant as the full moon, contrasting with, and giving unrivalled intensity to, large black eyes, black as night, and luxuriant raven locks, entered the room.

Since the scene which I am attempting to describe, I have travelled much. I have seen the fair daughters of Europe; I have beheld the dark-eyed, impassioned Italian, the majestic beauty of Rome, as well as the softer and more feminine Florentine; I have seen the sprightly belles of France, those proud arbiters of fashion, who dictate the laws of costume to the rest of that quarter of the globe; and I have seen the women of England, who, beyond a doubt, if nature allowed of emulation in such cases, might fairly claim to be models of beauty to the rest of their sex. All these have I seen. I nevertheless can scarcely call to my recollection any individual whom I could regard as equal, and still less, superior in charms, to one of these children of the mountain; so far, at least, as mere physical requisites go to the constitution of female loveliness.

      *   *   *   *   *

      *   *   *   *   *

The three jairiahs now approached us, and one
of them, going upon one knee, presented the
" lakan," a round tunnel-shaped vessel of silver-
gilt, with a cover pierced full of holes, and having
around it receptacles for soap, for the purpose of
washing. A second slave, also kneeling, held in
her hand a silver-gilt vase, or urn, of exquisite
workmanship, containing water, which she continued to pour on the " lakan," through the holes in
the cover of which it fell into the vessel beneath,
until we had completed our ablutions. A third
held the napkins, the edges of which were embroidered with gold.

This ceremony performed, two other jairiahs appeared, each having a " bakhour," or censer, with
two handles, filled with incense, which shed a delicious perfume throughout the apartment. These
were followed by three others; one of whom bore
a silver-gilt tray, on which were placed six gold
cups of exquisite workmanship, containing three
different sorts of sherbet, which were handed to
us by a second jairiah; whilst a third held in her
hand a napkin embroidered with gold. Then
came three others; one bearing a tray of gold,
inlaid with diamonds and emeralds, on which

were small china cups, called "fingan," together
with vessels, or holders of gold, embossed and
jewelled, called "zerf," serving for saucers. These
are used to protect the hands from burning; as
the coffee, which is made exceedingly strong, and
drunk without milk or sugar, is taken so hot, that
it would be impossible to hold the vessel actually
containing it.

The coffee having been removed, two eunuchs
entered, bearing in their hands the "nerghila,"
or pipe, most commonly in use among the ladies
of Mesopotamia. It is not unlike the hookah in
design, except that the vessel containing the rose-
water is in the form of a globe, and the tube
between the mouth-piece and the reservoir of
rose-water is rigid instead of being flexible. The
soothing influence of the " nerghila," the fragrance
of the burning aloe, the gentle murmuring of the
rose-water in the reservoir, and the tender strains
issuing from a musical box brought from Europe,
which poured forth clusters of notes, clear and
distinct as the dripping of a fountain in the noon-
day shade, combined to lull our senses into a state
of happiness, like that produced by a delicious
dream.

I believe it will be long before the ladies of
Europe will participate with me in my enthusiasm for tobacco; although they have pretty generally adopted a custom derived from a country
still nearer the rising sun; I mean that of tea-
drinking. Never shall I forget the astonishment
depicted in the countenances of the passers-by,
when, having dined at Richmond with a party of
friends, I was walking in the Park, after dinner,
leaning on the arm of a German gentleman, who
was smoking a cigar himself, and had the politeness to offer me one, which, I confess, I had not
the fortitude to refuse. They looked as much
surprised as we in the East should be to behold a
man without hair on the upper lip.

During the half hour in which we were enjoying our " nerghilahs" we conversed but little. Ten
jairiahs stood before us, in an attitude of respect,
with their arms reverentially folded before them.
Our pipes being finished, the Pasha's sister offered
to show me her brother's harem; a proposal to
which my curiosity gave a ready assent.

We proceeded first to visit the bed-rooms;
which were very numerous. They were covered,

for the most part, with magnificent carpets. The beds, the manufacture of Bagdad, were made of the branches of the palm-tree, and were so light, that the whole frame might, without difficulty, be lifted with one hand. On the bed of the Pasha's chief wife were five matrasses, each covered with silk of a different colour from the others, filled with the feathers of the peacock.

After seeing a number of sleeping-rooms fitted up in this manner, which could not have been fewer than thirty, we ascended to the terrace on the roof, from which we enjoyed a fine view of the whole town and its environs, mingled, here and there, with the mouldering ruins of the once mighty city of Nineveh. While I was gazing upon them, how forcibly did the words of the Prophet present themselves to my mind—" And as for Nineveh her waters are like a great pool; but the men flee away. They cry: stand, stand, but there is none that will return back. Take ye the spoil of the silver, take ye the spoil of the gold: for there is no end of the riches of all the precious furniture. She is destroyed, and rent and torn; the heart melteth and the knees

fail, and all the loins lose their strength; and the
faces of them all are as the blackness of a kettle.
* * * Behold I come against thee, saith the Lord
of Hosts; and I will burn thy chariots even to
smoke, and the sword shall devour thy young
lions; and I will cut off thy prey out of the
land, and the voice of thy messengers shall be
heard no more. Thy shepherds have slumbered,
O king of Assyria; thy princes shall be buried:
thy people are hid in the mountains, and there is
none to gather them together."

On the roof were erected three tents, made
of a blueish-green oilcloth. Protected by these
we enjoyed the magnificent prospect before us,
unmolested by the rays of the sun. After remaining here for a short time, we descended
into the garden, which covered an immense
space of ground, not less, I should say, than
three-quarters of a square mile, intersected on
every side with rivulets of water, of not more
than a foot in width, embanked with marble, and
fringed with a profusion of flowers of every description, which filled the surrounding air with
fragrance; the predominating odour proceeding

from the beds of roses, which flourished in most
lavish abundance.

After spending an hour in this enchanting place,
the princess conducted me to a saloon opening
upon the garden, where I was introduced to the
wives of her brother, the Pasha, in number twenty-
five. In addition to Georgians and Circassians,
there were some from Kurdistan. One of them,
with whom I conversed, was a beautiful Georgian,
with large black eyes, shaded by eye-lashes, long,
dark, and drooping like a cedar branch, and not
more than eighteen years old. She told me she
was born of Christian parents, and that at the age
of twelve she had been carried off to Constanti-
nople, where she had been compelled, on pain of
death, to abjure her faith and embrace that of Islam.
She had a brother, a Mamaluke, in the service of
the Pasha, who had also been forced to abjure the
faith of his fathers. I asked her if she was happy
in her present condition? she replied, that, far from
rejoicing at her lot, she never ceased to bewail her
hard fate, and to mourn the loss of parents and
kindred.

Our colloquy was here cut short by the entrance

of the Pasha himself. All instantly rose to salute
him. He was a man apparently about forty years
of age, and of lofty and commanding stature:
his eyes were large, dark, and brilliant; his beard,
which was black and copious, descended to his
girdle, where his " hanjar," or dagger hung, its
handle rough, and sparkling with jewels. His
dress was sumptuous and befitting his rank, and
his courteous manner inspired confidence and
respect.

The princess presented me to him as the rela-
tive of his " kerkhea," or lieutenant, which was the
fact; whereupon he received me with distinguished
politeness, and made many inquiries respecting my
family and kindred, particularly after my father,
who was at that time at Bassorah, on his way to
Bagdad. Our conversation had lasted a quarter
of an hour, when the mollah, from the minaret,
began to call all true believers to the " salat al
zohor," or mid-day prayer, whereupon the Pasha
immediately took his leave, for the purpose of
repairing to the adjoining mosque, leaving his
" harem " to say their prayers in the saloon.

This summons is repeated five times during the
day: at daybreak the mollah calls all true mussul-

mans to their devotions, with the words, "prayer
is better than sleep;" the summons to the salat al
zohor, or mid-day prayer, is, "prayer is better
than food;" the third call, at three o'clock, and is
named "el assr;" the fourth, called "el mug-
gerib," takes place at sunset; and the fifth at
midnight.

Forthwith the ladies gave themselves up to their
devotions; first going upon their knees, and then
prostrating themselves on the ground, and kissing it, crying aloud, "There is no God but Allah!
there is no God but the God of heaven, and Mahomet is his prophet; there is no hope, no refuge,
save in the most high and mighty God." During
all this time they had before them what they called
a relique of the great Prophet himself, which was
no less than a fragment of the very "sherwals," or
trowsers, said to have graced the limbs of Mahomet's sister, enveloped in paper, and encased in a
rich gold cover, inlaid with diamonds. This precious relique they repeatedly kissed, and placed
on their heads during their prayers.

These pious observances lasted about a quarter
of an hour, during the whole of which period I
remained seated on the "diwan," regarding the

extraordinary scene with unmingled curiosity.   As
soon as it was over, a slave entered and announced
dinner.   The invitation was promptly attended to,
and we all proceeded to the dining-room, which, on
account of the great heat of the weather (it being
then the month of June) was one of the apartments opening, the whole width of one of its
sides, into the court.

As many of my readers may be unacquainted
with the detail of Oriental gastronomy, I will
briefly describe some of the *haut-gouts* served up
on the occasion of my visit to the palace of the
Pasha of Mosul.   First of all a tray, containing
twenty dishes, was brought in and placed upon a
large round salver or stand, of copper, about six
feet in diameter.   Among these dishes were soups,
one made of rice and herbs, the other with green
corn and chickens, a favourite dish of the present
Pasha of Egypt.

Amongst the dishes which succeeded to these
were a lamb, stuffed with all sorts of herbs, rice,
and pistachios, which was served up whole, saffron
being added, for the double purpose of giving it
colour and flavour; a number of roast fowls: stuffed
gourds; two or three large dishes of a vegetable,

called " bamia;" and a dish made of a veal hash,
enveloped in vine leaves; " coobba," which is a
crust made of green corn and hashed meat, filled
with a hash of beef and herbs, called ": shar al
ajouz," or old woman's hair, of delicious flavour,
and made up into globes, as large as a man's head ;
many dishes of " kabap," or " kabob," as it is more
usually written, which is a kind of sausage meat,
cooked on an iron rod; together with a host of
other recondite preparations, the names of which
have passed from my memory.

When the solid portion of the dinner had been
disposed of, a profusion of sweetmeats, of the most
delicious flavour, were put upon the table, and with
which the repast concluded. Of course, no wine
was introduced; but we managed to console ourselves with drinking a liquor made from the juice
of the pomegranate, which was handed to us in
goblets of massive gold.

During the whole time of dinner, fifteen slaves
were in attendance, some of whom fanned us continually. Having brought in the necessary vessels
for the performance of our ablutions, and accom-
modated us with our pipes and nerghilahs, they
were permitted to withdraw, and regale themselves

on the remains of our repast. I had almost forgotten to mention the "nuckel," or dessert, which,
in its way, was in no wise inferior to the dinner.
There was a substance having the consistency of
snow, which is found on the leaves of trees, of a
green colour, having a delicious sweet taste, called
in the Chaldean language "gasgoul," and in Arabic
"man al sama." There were also the figs of Jebel
Sinjar (a mountain to the northwest of Mosul,) of
enormous size, some of them being not less than
six inches in length; the "laimoun halou," or
sweet orange, from Bagdad and Bassorah, a fruit
almost as large as a shaddock, greatly resembling
the orange in size and appearance, but far excelling
that fruit in smoothness of skin and sweetness of
flavour. So abundant is this fruit in Mesopotamia
that twelve are sold for a penny. "Hammas," a sort
of kernel, resembling a dried harvest bean, which
is roasted after the manner of coffee; to which
may be added pistachio nuts, pomegranates, and
grapes.

The repast finished, we were conducted upstairs
to the "tharma," an apartment on the first floor,
corresponding, in some manner, with the Iwān
below. It was paved with marble, and looked out

upon the gardens.   In the centre of the room was placed the " serrir," a large ottoman, covered with yellow satin, on which reclined the chief wife of the Pasha, and around which several cushions were ranged.   On the side, towards the garden, were hung a number of cages, filled with beautiful sing-ing-birds, sending forth notes of every description.

In this earthly paradise we enjoyed our " ner-ghilahs" and sipped our coffee.   This being over, the sultana, or favourite wife of the Pasha, com-posed herself to sleep, according to the Oriental fashion ; an amiable weakness which, I greatly fear, is not calculated to secure for my illustrious friend the approval of her own sex in this colder climate, where, as I have been given to under-stand, the practice of taking a nap after dinner is confined almost entirely to elderly agas, who have laughed at the beard of the prophet, by partaking of the condemned juice of the grape.

A fair slave stood at the head of her still fairer mistress, and watched her slumbers, waiving to and fro a broad fan made of peacock's feathers.   An-other attendant was occupied in chafing her small and delicately white feet, from which the slippers had been removed ;   whilst a   third   proceeded

to chaunt a low and melancholy strain, for the
purpose of inducing sleep, which, it must be
confessed, her song was admirably calculated to
promote.

For the information of my female readers I
will give a brief description of the dress worn
upon this occasion by the favoured fair one, entitled *par excellence* to pull the beard of the
much-dreaded Pasha of Mosul. The moment is
favourable, for the fair sultana sleeps, and is unconscious that I am disclosing her charms to the
gaze of profane kafirs. Well, then, her " khamis," or
chemise, was of the finest white silk gossamer, over
which was a " ghombaz" of white silk, embroidered
with flowers of gold.   Her " sherwals," or trousers,
were of crimson: round her waist was a girdle of
ribbon covered with the richest embroidery, the
work of the " jairiahs," or white female slaves; who
have erroneously been supposed to pass their whole
lives in unmitigated idleness.   This girdle was
profusely studded over with precious stones, and
fastened in the middle by a gold clasp, carved into
a device representing two pigeons; the heads of
which were set with jewels.   On her arms were

bracelets, having alternate rows of pearls and diamonds. Her "kirdan," or necklace, was composed
of gold, and of precious stones of various kinds.
In her ears were pendants, formed of brilliants of
dazzling lustre; and in her nose, fastened in a little
hole on the right side—faint not, ye daughters of
Europe—in her nose was a small emerald. Her
hair, which was combed back off her forehead, was
arranged in an infinity of small braids, confined
and adorned by chains of gold and pearls, each
braid divided into three or four branches or tails,
each of which terminated in a single pearl; while
two braids, also decorated with pearls and gold,
graced either cheek. These, with an ornament
of gold, somewhat in the form of a saucer, and an
aigrette of diamonds, representing a bird, completed her head-dress.

Near her was placed her favourite "durrah," or
parrot, of which a most marvellous anecdote was
narrated to me. The bird had, it seems, been
taught to pronounce divers sentences from the
Koran, and had arrived at such a proficiency in
his pious exercises as almost to rival the Mollah
himself in his devout ejaculations. It is the lot of

the faithful to undergo trials: and accordingly it
so fell out one day that an irreverent bird of prey
happened to espy the feathered devotee, who, absorbed, no doubt, in pious meditation, and wholly
unconscious of danger, was wandering at some distance from its cage. Not having the fear of Mahomet before its eyes, the ill-omened bird, who, if
not a downright western kafir, must have been either
a shiah or yezidi, no sooner espied the wanderer,
than, without the smallest ceremony, he pounced
on the loquacious friend of the beautiful sultana,
and ascended some distance with her into the air,
with the full intention of making a hearty meal;
when the parrot forthwith exclaimed, in loud
accents—" La illahoun ila Allah w', Mohammed
rasul Allah."—" There is but one God and Mahomet is his prophet."

Upon hearing this, the bird of prey began to
have his misgivings; but when the parrot continued,
in the same pious strain, " all the rest is vanity of
vanities," it became clear to his mind, that he had
got himself into an awkward predicament. He
therefore lost no time in ridding himself of his unwelcome burthen, and as the only amends which

he had in his power to make, very politely
brought him down again, placed him close to his
cage, and went his way. As for the "durrah"
he obtained, from that time forward, a character
of high sanctity, and was ever after regarded by
the servants of the Pasha and all the harem as the
especial protegé of the prophet. Such was the tale
related to me by the princess.

The sultana having arisen from her slumbers,
accompanied the princess, the serrari, and myself,
in a stroll round the garden; where we regaled
ourselves by chewing a mineral of a greenish
colour called "alk," found near Nineveh, which
has an agreeable taste and smell, and does not
dissolve in the mouth. It is supposed to have the
property of assisting the digestion.

Shortly after, the mollah proclaimed the "salat
el assr," or evening prayer. Upon which, I obtained, from my distinguished hostess, permission
to leave the palace. She was very loth to part
with me, and proposed that we should, at an early
day, make an excursion together to the tomb of
the prophet Jonas; who is held in high reverence
both by Christians and Infidels. This tomb is

situated a short distance from Mosul, on a mountain called Tel nabbi Yunus.

Although nothing would have pleased me more
than to have accompanied the princess on so
agreeable an excursion, I was compelled to decline
her invitation, in consequence of the illness of my
mother, who was suffering from a complaint from
which she invariably obtained speedy relief, by resorting to the hot springs of Ain el Kibrit, which
are situated at a short distance from Mosul, on
the banks of the Tigris, towards Bagdad, and are
reckoned efficacious in curing a great variety of
diseases. The princess, to tempt me to abandon
my determination, told me that her brother had
just purchased a little Kurd slave, of exquisite
beauty, from the mountains of Sinjar, a place between Mosul and Diarbekir. She could speak
no language but that of Kurdistan, and the princess, knowing that I understood it, expected thus
to excite my curiosity. My mother, however, had
made it a point that I should accompany her on
her journey, and I had, therefore, no alternative
but to decline the proffered honour.

As it was late when I quitted the Pasha's palace,

I did not return to my home, the convent, that
evening, but took up my night's abode at the house
of a married sister of mine, who resided at no
great distance from the palace, near the mosque
Nour el din.

CHAPTER IV.

The Baths of Ain el Kibrit—Extraordinary abundance of Food
—Travelling Bakers—Mode of Preparing Corn—Mode of
Building Houses—Eastern Hospitality—Worshippers of the
Devil—Mesopotamian Marriages—Remarkable Charm—A
Modern Miracle—Singular Sport—An Adventure in the
Desert—Churches of the Oriental Christians.

SHORTLY after the visit described in the last
chapter, I started in company with my mother for
the baths of Ain el Kibrit. After a journey of
three hours, during which nothing of importance
occurred, we reached the place of our destination,
and pitched our tents without having met with the
slightest interruption from the marauding tribes
that swarm in these parts.

To a person of a curious turn of mind, Ain el
Kibrit presents a variety of attractions. It is
there that the substance called "alk," which I
have just described, is found; and it was one of
my usual amusements while there, to sally forth

for the purpose of collecting it. Hard by the fountain which has made this spot so great a resort for invalids, stands a mountain called " Kurkur-baba," from the top of which, a vapour issues upon digging a little way down, which bursts into flame on coming in contact with the atmosphere. This we turned to account in cooking our pillaus, and the boiling of water.

From my infancy I had always a large share of that attribute of my sex, curiosity; and I remember on one occasion I nearly fell a martyr to my passion for scientific investigation, by too nearly approaching the flame issuing from this mountain. The fire is readily extinguished. A small quantity of earth thrown upon it quenches it instantly, by closing the aperture whence it issues. From this mountain also issue three sources of naptha, which descend into the plain. If a piece of cotton or cloth is thrown into one of them alight, a terrific explosion takes place, like the discharge of a cannon; the stream is enveloped in smoke, until the obnoxious substance is entirely consumed, when it resumes its accustomed appearance.

A bituminous fountain has also its rise in this mountain; into which, if any person should imprudently venture, he would, in all probability, pay the forfeit of his life for his rashness, as it would be impossible for him to disengage himself from its tenacious grasp.

After staying at the baths until my mother's health was perfectly re-established, we set out for Telkef, a town about nine miles distant from Mosul, towards Amadieh, of which my uncle was governor. The town is pleasantly situated, as its name, which signifies "the mountain of delight," imports, and the soil is good, producing nearly every sort of fruit and vegetable, to be found in that latitude. Carrots a yard in length and six inches in diameter have been grown there, and of so great a weight, that a child would be unable to carry one of them. Turnips are also produced, sometimes two feet in diameter, which are eaten both raw and cooked in various ways; and a kind of cucumber, resembling a huge serpent, is also grown here. The latter is most frequently seen in a horse-shoe shape, and is so long that when put round the neck the two ends nearly reach the knees. It is a very common practice with the natives to pickle the turnip in vinegar; and in this state it is much used as a stimulus to languid

appetites, or when the system, from heat or any
other cause, has become feverish.

Besides the vegetables I have enumerated, they
have the "battikh," or water melon, which grows
to an enormous size, grapes as large as walnuts,
and apples in such abundance, that they may be
had almost for the asking. An European upon one
occasion wishing to purchase a para's worth of
them, was asked by the seller, if he had brought
a basket to put them into. Now, a para being of
no more value than an English farthing, the European, when he beheld the enormous store into the
possession of which he had been put by this small
investment of capital, opened his eyes with wonder,
and exclaimed—" Of a truth this is the land of
promise !"

Neither is this extraordinary abundance, and
consequent cheapness, confined to vegetables and
fruits : for, in the neighbourhood of Telkef, a large
sheep may be purchased for three piastres, about
two shillings English ; and a chicken for three
paras, which is little more than three farthings.
Money, however, seldom makes its appearance in
these transactions ; which are, in nearly every
case, carried on by simple barter : each inhabitant

devoting his land and labour to one or more kinds of produce, which he exchanges for that of his neighbour.

The bread made there is white and of excellent quality. It usually sells at the rate of four or five paras, about a penny farthing English, the " ratel," which is about equal to five pounds English weight. But though it is held in high estimation by the Arabs, I doubt whether this bread would be equally palatable to an European taste, from its being mixed with various kinds of odoriferous herbs and salt. It is made by a class of Bedouin women, called " khabazāt," who make a regular calling of it; going their rounds from village to village, and staying a short time in each. The dough, after having been kneaded, is rolled out into cakes of about three feet in circumference, but not more than half an inch in thickness, and then baked in the oven. It retains its freshness for a whole month. The corn, before it is ground, is carefully cleansed from dirt and all impurity. When well kneaded, the bread is baked in the following manner. The oven is built of brick, and is of a round conical form, decreasing in diameter towards the mouth, somewhat resem-

bling a well in shape. It rises from the floor of
the bakehouse to about the height of an ordinary
sized man's waist. It does not rise vertically from
the floor, but at an angle, leaning outwards from
the wall against which it is built towards the
person engaged in baking. In the bottom of this
oven, which is usually about seven feet in diameter,
is a furnace, which is fixed below the level of the
floor. The oven being well heated, the khabāzat
takes a piece of dough, previously rolled out and
fashioned into the form of a large round disk, and
covering her hand with a machine made of rushes,
stuffed with hay and covered with oilcloth, to
prevent it from burning, plasters the dough against
the side of the oven, which holds six loaves. In two
minutes the batch is baked, and removed to make
room for another, to which a third succeeds, until
the desired quantity is completed. In an hour a
mountain of bread is made by this process. When
brought to table, the bread is placed on a round
rush mat, and damped with water to make it
pliant, and is then eaten with either pieces of
meat, cheese, or olives, enveloped in it. Five
women are employed in these operations, which
are never performed by men. So expert are these

peripatetic bakers in their calling, that in the course of one day, they will make a quantity sufficient to fill the "sella," or bread store—a vast chamber, in which stands a round structure made of wicker work, about nine feet in diameter, and four feet high, the manufacture of the poor Nestorians, who dwell in the desolate mountains of Zozane.

While I am upon this subject, I am naturally led to speak of the mode adopted in Mesopotamia for thrashing and winnowing corn; which is altogether different from that pursued in those European countries, in which I have had the opportunity of witnessing the operation. I have not seen the English process; but the Italian mode, of which I have frequently been a witness, appears to me unhandy, unnecessarily laborious, and much inferior to that practised in my native country. The method pursued in Mesopotamia, or at least those parts of it in the neighbourhood of Mosul, is as follows.

Telkef is renowned for the enormous height to which the corn growing in the surrounding fields attains. The stalk grows to such a length that a horseman can ride through a field without being seen, the point of his lance alone peering above the waving ears.

The corn is cut about mid-way between the ear and the root; the stalk being left to furnish fodder for the camels and other beasts of burthen. I think I remember to have seen it asserted in some book, that the corn is pulled up by the roots with the hand, in my country, after the manner to which allusion is supposed to be made in the Bible. I can only say, that I never witnessed such a practice. The narrator was possibly deceived by seeing the weeds plucked up in this manner. The corn being cut, the proprietor of the field is forbidden to touch what remains, by an express law, which makes the gleaning sacred to the poor. So abundant is the produce, in comparison with the wants of the inhabitants, that a large measure of corn, containing from ten to fifteen ratel, or from fifty to seventy pounds English weight, is, in good seasons, sold for three piastres.

Harvest being over, the produce of the district is gathered in the desert; where it is heaped up into a vast mass, having the appearance of a moderately sized hill, on which are placed men, who keep up a constant supply to the machine used for separating the ear from the straw and husk. As I have never, during my travels, seen an apparatus in any degree resembling the one used in Mesopotamia and Assyria, for this purpose, I will attempt briefly to describe it.

A wooden cylinder, about four feet long and two feet thick, is fixed horizontally under a platform which rests on a carriage, mounted on wheels. On this cylinder, which revolves like a wheel, at an interval of about one foot, are fixed two rows of sharp blades, somewhat in the shape of hatchet heads. These turn within four inches of the ground. The whole machine is yoked to two or more horses, according to the quantity of corn and the means of the district, and is then drawn round in a circle of vast diameter: the driver standing on the platform, which is raised about three or four feet from the ground. During the whole of the time a constant supply of corn is furnished by the labourers on the heap in the centre, who manage to throw it exactly in the course of the machine, where it is completely

crushed by the revolving cylinder, until the whole
heap has undergone the operation.

On the outside of this huge circle are stationed
a number of men, who, with an instrument which,
in some degree, answers the purpose of a rake,
though it differs widely in appearance from that
implement, having the teeth arranged in circles,
one above another, not altogether unlike a birch
broom, gather the crushed corn; which is then
winnowed in the most simple manner, by throwing it into the air, and allowing the chaff to blow
away.

The ears being separated from the chaff, are
again gathered together in a large pile, on which
the "nazur," who is an officer appointed by the
Pasha of the district, for the purpose of securing
the share of the produce due to the government,
imprints his own name in large characters. This
act he performs in several parts of the heap: so
that to carry any away before the Pasha has taken
his share, which amounts to a tenth part of the
whole produce, without detection, becomes impossible. These precautions, together with the dread
of five hundred lashes, the penalty affixed to this
offence, combine to secure to the government, or

at least to its representative, its full share of the
produce. The nazur having taken his due, the
rest becomes the lawful possession of the grower.
By the process I have above described, a vast
quantity of corn is thrashed and winnowed, in an
incredibly short space of time.

Each corn-field contains several vast wells,
about twenty feet deep, of a conical form, being
about three feet in diameter at the mouth, which
is on a level with the ground, and about ten feet
in diameter at the bottom. The bottom and sides
are thickly coated with the bitumen which is so
abundant in these parts, so that it is impossible
for the moisture from the earth to penetrate.
Into these receptacles the surplus produce of each
year is cast, to be taken out in case of need, or to
supply traders in corn, who happen to arrive in any
of the numerous caravans passing from time to
time through the district. The top is covered in
securely by means of a large round stone; and the
corn is taken out, when required, by letting down a
man by means of ropes, with a large basket, which
he fills with the grain until the requisite quantity
is obtained. It is by no means uncommon for vast
quantities of this stored produce to be destroyed,

when, by a succession of favourable seasons, the
supply has so far outgrown all possible demand,
that the article becomes a mere incumbrance.
How many might this surplus produce save from
starvation, if man would but direct all his energies
to the welfare of his fellow creatures !

The quantity required for the year's consumption is taken home by each proprietor, and stored
in the shekhim, as the corn-store is called in my
country.   This is the space left at the top of the
house under the terrace.   The terrace, it is well
known, is flat, and supported by a sort of dome, so
that a large vacant space is necessarily left under
each corner of the flat roof; and it is in these
vacant spaces that the year's supply of corn is
stowed away.   It is not usual to employ more
than two of these chambers, inasmuch as this
number is generally found amply sufficient to
contain the annual provision.   In the chambers
underneath there is a hole in the wall, which is
stopped with a plug of cloth; and, when a supply
of corn is needed, the plug is taken out; and a
sack, placed under the aperture, receives the grain,
which leaps forth as from a fountain and speedily
fills it.

The town of Telkef contains about 20,000 inhabitants, who, with very few exceptions, are Christians. The houses are built in a solid manner, of stone, brought from neighbouring quarries, and joined by a cement made with lime, the produce of the same quarries; which, in a very short space of time, dries, and becomes as hard as the stone itself.

Their mode of building is remarkable, and, for expedition, surpasses any thing I ever saw; for, in the space of three or four days, they will contrive to finish a substantial house, consisting of two or three stories. The materials having been prepared before hand, a number of workmen assemble, and are then divided into two parties. One is engaged in placing the stone in layers, one above the other, whilst the others are occupied in slacking the lime, preparing the mortar, and handing it, when prepared, to the former party. It is absolutely necessary that these operations should proceed simultaneously; otherwise the mortar would be hardened before it could be applied to the surface of the stones.

No beams of wood of any kind are used in the construction of these dwellings, not even for the ceilings, which, like the rest of the building, are composed of stone, united by layers of mortar; the whole becoming, in half an hour, an almost homogeneous mass, of such solidity and strength, that the workmen, at the expiration of that time, are enabled to commence their operations for building the upper story, and place masses of stone, of great weight, on this recently erected stage.

In form, the houses of this town, do not materially differ from those found in most parts of Assyria and Mesopotamia, having arcades running round their inner court, both on the ground and the upper story. A cistern usually occupies the centre of the court, but no fountains are to be met with in these parts, with, perhaps, the single exception of those in the Pasha's palace. The houses, although built of stone, are generally coated over with the cement employed in uniting them. When dry it becomes as white as snow, and produces that dazzling effect, so often spoken of by travellers, upon viewing these towns from a distance, under the cloudless sky and brilliant sun of these regions.

Near this town is a fountain of tepid water, which continues of the same temperature both

in summer and winter, and has a pleasant taste.
not unlike *eau sucrée*. A quantity of large turtles
are found here; but this delicacy of London
Aldermen (as I am given to understand) is never
eaten by the inhabitants, who loathe it as they
loathe ass's flesh. All around it are to be discovered the ruins of ancient Nineveh.

It was here that my father established those
factories by which he sought to repair the ravages
to which his fortune had been subjected, on account of his unflinching adherence to the principles of his faith. Three of these were for the
purpose of extracting the oil from the seeds of
a plant called, in Arabic, simsim, an article
which has an enormous consumption there, being,
as well as the oil derived from the castor plant,
used for lamps. It also enters largely into the
domestic cookery of the inhabitants.

The mode of extracting it is as follows:—The
factory usually consists of four large chambers,
three of which are about forty feet square; the
other being of smaller dimensions. In one of
these, which is paved with asphalte obtained in
the neighbourhood, the seeds, having previously
been macerated a sufficient time in water, to render

them of the requisite softness, are crushed with
large wooden mallets, about four or five feet in
length, which are wielded by men, standing five
or six in a row, and perfectly naked, with the
exception of a belt.   During the whole time they
are engaged in this labour, they lighten their toil,
by singing in chorus to a monotonous see-saw sort
of melody, such sentences as the following:—
" God will help us : man is born to earn his bread
by the sweat of his brow."

The seeds being all crushed in this manner, the
pulp is disengaged from the husks, which present
a dark brown appearance, by washing, and is then
placed in a furnace and roasted, until it assumes a
brown colour; when it is put into a mill, worked
by horse-power, whence it issues, in the form of
a transparent paste of considerable consistency,
somewhat resembling the melted sugar used by
pastry-cooks in ornamental confectionary, in colour,
a yellowish white.   In this form it is commonly
eaten with honey, with which it makes a most
delicious compound.

The pulp being reduced to the state above
described, is then drawn off into another reservoir,
and thence, having been subjected to the action

of hot water, which is poured on it, it issues in a
state fit for general consumption. What remains
is generally given away to the poor, to whom,
when mixed with honey, it affords an agreeable
and nutritious kind of food. The residue is also
used as food for cattle, in fattening which it answers
the purpose of oil cake.

The inhabitants of Telkef are, as I before stated,
nearly all Christians, and observe the ordinances
of their religion with the greatest strictness in all
their primeval purity. Far from confining themselves to the mere profession of Christianity, or
contenting themselves with reading the sacred
books, at stated periods and at distant intervals,
they devote a part of every day to the study of
them, and their whole lives are passed in constant
endeavours to follow out their divine precepts.

Of the practical influence of their religion upon
their manners and conduct, I have been the
witness of almost super-human examples, in the
forgiveness of injuries, and the rendering of good
for evil. No dissimulation, nor concealed rancour,
rankles in the breasts of these simple-hearted
children of nature. The man who one moment is
heard applying to his fellow-man the most oppro-

brious term that can be applied by one man to
another "khanzir," meaning pig, which not unfrequently makes the hanjar leap out of its sheath,—
is seen the next embracing him on whom he has
vented his wrath, in perfectly good brotherhood.
The eastern blood is far too fiery to suppress the
emotions of anger. The heart of an Oriental
would burst if he attempted to smother his feelings; so that the worst is seen at once. An instance in which the influence of the religious
feeling was strikingly exemplified occurs to my
recollection. In the town of Telkef lived a woman
who had an only son, the prop and comfort
of her age. Scarcely had he attained to man-
hood, when, in one of those broils, unfortunately
common to every country, he was slain. His
murderer, an outcast on the world, without, as he
believed, friend or protector, found both in the
mother of his victim; in her, whose joy he had
turned into mourning, and whose habitation he
had made desolate. She pardoned, in order that
she herself, on the great day of judgment, might
obtain pardon at the hands of Him who, when he
came in great humility to teach mankind the way
to salvation, enjoined us strictly to forgive our

enemies, if we ourselves would obtain forgiveness.

Much attention is paid to education in this small community. It is difficult to meet with any person, male or female, who cannot both read and write. From the encouragement given to the useful arts and sciences, Telkef has not unfrequently been called little Athens. In no part of the world are the two great commandments of the law and the prophets more strictly obeyed: " Thou shalt love the Lord thy God with thy whole heart, and with thy whole soul, and with all thy strength, and with all thy mind, and thy neighbour as thyself." In such high esteem is chastity held among them, that they punish the violation of it by stoning the delinquent to death.

In Lent, the inhabitants of Telkef fast rigidly; subsisting entirely upon such vegetables as rice and truffles, which they eat sometimes roasted, and sometimes in soup. In thus alluding to the rigid adherence of the inhabitants of Telkef to the precepts of our religion, I by no means desire to claim for them a superiority over the Christians of Mosul and Mesopotamia in general. They are all remarkable for the patriarchal simplicity of their

lives. The exclamations "death is certain, but
the hour uncertain; for it shall come as a thief in
the night! life is even as the lightning's flash, and
all the riches, and pleasures, and honours of this
world are but vanity of vanities!" are ever in their
mouths, exerting a salutary influence over their
thoughts and actions.

Their habitations are plain. They are not
anxious to acquire riches, save with the view of
dispensing charity, and rendering acceptable service to their fellow-creatures. Neither is that
charity restricted by intolerance to those of our
faith. Their bounty and their good offices are
extended to all who are in want or tribulation, be
they Jews or Gentiles, Mahometans or Yezidis.
"Cast," say they, "thy bread upon the running
waters; for after a long time thou shalt find it
again. Of all that is given in charity, God, who
feedeth the fowls of the air, will keep account."

Whether Christian or Mahometan, hospitality is
considered by every dweller in Arabia as the most
sacred duty of humanity. Disputes had frequently
happened among neighbouring Christian families,
as to which of the two should have the privilege,
for such they considered it, of entertaining the

stranger. In consequence of this, a law was
made among them, that he who should first touch
the stranger should become his host. Nor do
they consider that in so doing they are performing
an act of exalted virtue; on the contrary, they
only regard it as the operation of an instinct implanted in the bosom of man, for the promotion of
his own happiness, and that of his fellow-creatures.
" The kindly fruits of the earth," they say, " were
sent for the comfort of all the sons of Adam."
Even the Bedouins, those wandering shedders of
blood, who assert, by divine sanction, their privilege to rob and to kill, and with whom the life of
a human being is of no more account than that of
a bull or a ram, acknowledge the sacredness of this
obligation

To their table no invitation is needed; the want
of a meal being the only necessary qualification;
nor do they think it indispensable to inquire first
into the birth and parentage of their guest, and of
his ability to return the obligation. The stranger
enters, takes his seat at the board, and consumes his
share of the good things, of which there is seldom
any stint, almost as a matter of right. What remains is never saved for the morrow, but given

away to the poor. A sour look at the unexpected appearance of a stranger or acquaintance at the dinner hour, which, I am given to understand, is by no means an uncommon thing on European countenances, is in Assyria unknown. Only in the hour of death do they regard with displeasure the entrance of a friend or stranger.

My father was distinguished for the extent to which he carried his charity. He spent no inconsiderable part of his once ample fortune in the exercise of that virtue, which he sometimes carried to an extreme bordering upon enthusiasm. Not satisfied with relieving the unfortunate individuals who made direct application to him, he has frequently been known to sally forth in quest of objects on whom he might exercise his benevolence. Sometimes he would even bring them home with him, place them at his table, give them of the best he had, and attend upon them himself. Nay, more; he would even wash their feet, and taking off their rags, clothe them in his own garments. This I have seen him repeatedly do; and, ardent and elevated as my notions were, I confess I sometimes thought he was carrying the virtue beyond its extreme verge.

It was no uncommon thing for him to purchase negro women, who, from age and infirmity, had become incapable of work, in order to preserve them, in their declining years, from neglect and ill-treatment. This conduct excited, I well remember, the merriment of a Kurd chief, a friend of my father, from the neighbouring mountain of Sinjar, who asked him what on earth he could want with such old hags? My father answered, " Li Wigi Allah,"—" It is all for the face of God."

This Kurd chief, like many more, indeed the majority of those who inhabit the mountains of Sinjar, belonged to the religious sect called Yezidis, who worship the devil. I remember my father punishing me severely on one occasion, for spitting on the ground in the presence of this man; an act which is considered by the Yezidis as one of the grossest insults that can be offered to the evil one.

They make the sign of the cross, and administer the rite of baptism, after the manner of the oriental Christians, eight days after birth. They believe in a Supreme Being, and in Jesus Christ, to whom, like ourselves, they attribute the character of a Saviour. They embrace the rays of the rising

sun, and torches, candles, and all artificial means
of procuring light being regarded by them as impious, their use is strictly prohibited. It is a grave
offence against their religion to spit in the fire,
which they venerate as a sacred element. As I
have already observed, they worship the evil one,
whom they commonly call Amir el Zallām (the
Prince of Darkness). They make vows to him,
and cast votive offerings, sometimes of great value,
such as gold and jewels, into a deep pit in the
mountains of Sinjar. This circumstance coming to
the knowledge of certain Turkish authorities, they
compelled the chief priests of the Yezidis to disclose to them the situation of the sacred chasm, and
quickly transferring his satanic majesty's hoard to
their own coffers, I have no doubt used it in a
manner as satisfactory to that prince as though he
himself had been alone concerned in its distribution.

These wild enthusiasts are held in great dread,
from their remorseless cruelty towards those who
are so unfortunate as to fall into their hands. They
are terrible thieves, and never fail to attack caravans passing through the country they infest,
treating the ill-fated travellers whom they have
fleeced with extreme barbarity. They detest the

very name of Mahomet, and always single out his
followers as objects for the exercise of their refined cruelties; believing that by putting them to
death, more especially a sheriff, or descendant of
the prophet, they obtain a sure passport to the
realms of eternal bliss—a welcome entrance to
their " Jannah," or Paradise. All who happen
to die by the hands of Mahometans, are supposed to
have earned the crown of martyrdom ; a feeling
which is heartily reciprocated by the Turks, who
never neglect the opportunity of putting to death
a Yezidi.

For Christians, or rather for Christian churches
and monasteries, they entertain much respect; but
I never could learn that Christians ever escaped
robbery and ill-treatment, when they happened to
form part of a caravan attacked by these desperadoes. Upon entering a monastery, they take off
their shoes, and manifest their veneration by
kissing the walls of the sacred building. Into a
mosque they will never enter. So fearful are they
of giving offence to their prince, or " emir," the
great sheikh, as they call the Prince of Darkness, that
they exclude from their language all words having
the remotest resemblance to the sound of his name.

Like most enthusiasts, they are not without their scriptural texts in support of their doctrines, and place great reliance on that in which the evil one is said to have taken our Saviour to the top of a high mountain, and there to have offered him dominion over the whole world, if he would but fall down and worship him. From this circumstance they argue, that the government of the world must necessarily reside in Satan; and they therefore worship him, it is to be supposed, rather with a view to the deprecation of his wrath, than in admiration of his beneficent attributes. Like other theological disputants, they know where to stop in their quotations from Scripture: otherwise, one would suppose, the reply of our Saviour might have tended to unsettle their faith.

They are considered to be the descendants of the Manicheans. They have their priests and spiritual pastors; the chief of whom is supposed to enjoy the high honour and privilege of holding direct communication with his infernal majesty himself. This pontiff they invariably consult before they set about any enterprise of importance. Beyond this outline I have not been able to obtain any information respecting their tenets; seeing

that they are remarkably shy in their communi-
cations on the subject to unbelievers. They have
a church to which they resort, where they annually
hold a grand festival, and all of their sect, from far
and near, assemble. This holy city is said to be
in the mountains of Kurdistan.

From the great variety observable in their complexions and in the colour of their hair, they appear
to be a mixed race. In general they are of lofty
stature and symmetrical proportions. Those who
dwell in the mountains never trim their hair or
beards; which gives them a most uncouth and
ferocious appearance, entirely corresponding with
their habits of life.

Many attempts have been made by different
Pashas to put down these bands of marauders; but
hitherto they have proved unsuccessful. My father
often entertained them at his table; for, pious
Christian as he was, and surpassed by none in
the strict observance of all the ordinances of his
religion, he felt that, by so doing, he was best
imitating, with all humility, the example of his
heavenly teacher, who did not disdain to break
bread with publicans and sinners.

The forms observed in contracting marriages,

and the ceremonies performed upon their celebration, by the Christians of Mesopotamia, differ
widely from the practice pursued, in similar cases,
by those of Europe. Betrothals are frequently
made by parents immediately after the birth of
their children, who are not permitted to behold
each other till the day of marriage When a
woman has attained the age of twenty-one, she is
looked upon as completely *passée*, and is considered to have no longer any chance of obtaining
a husband.

The dower is provided by the husband. The
wife, even though she may be the daughter of a
prince, brings nothing but her ornaments and a
few personal trifling effects; whereas the husband
has to provide presents for the father, mother,
relations, and friends of his bride, besides paying
all incidental expenses. Upon the death of the
wife's father, however, the husband becomes entitled to her share of her parent's property.

Upon the day appointed for the nuptials, the
bridegroom, at an early hour, proceeds, accompanied by as many of his friends as he can collect
together, to the house of the father of his affianced
bride. Having received the blessing of the offi-

ciating priest, they sally forth, in a grand cavalcade, consisting of two divisions; of which the
bridegroom on horseback, his bridesmen, his friends
and relations, form one; and the bride, who is also
on horseback and closely veiled, with her relations,
friends, and attendants, the other. Besides those
especially invited to take part in the ceremony,
there is always a large concourse of acquaintances
and well-wishers, who accompany the procession
on foot.

Thus attended, they proceed round the town
or village in which the parents of the contracted
party reside, singing alleluias and spiritual songs;
which, in their turn, give place to the clang of
cymbals and the roll of tambours; while horns
and trumpets from their brazen mouths send forth
blasts which rend the air. Onward they proceed,
singing and rejoicing, every one breathing a benediction on the heads of the two whose lot is soon
to be indissoluble, so long as their earthly career
shall endure. The heart of every one present
beats with affection towards his fellow man. Envy,
hatred, and malice are banished from every breast.

But hush! They approach a church. The
tambour ceases to roll; the clang of the cymbal is

unheard; the trumpet is as silent as the grave;
the shouts which, ever and anon, burst from that
joyous throng, are heard no more, and are succeeded by strains of devout adoration and reverential awe. The church is passed. Again commence the shouts of joy, and hymns of exultation.

Amidst so much happiness the poor are not forgotten; paras descend in showers from the hands
of one of the bridesmen, who performs the grateful
office of almoner, and, from a basket affixed to
the pummel of his saddle, distributes the small but
acceptable coin to the surrounding spectators.

Thus carolling and hymning, they proceed to
the bridegroom's house ; against the door of which
they dash a porcelain vessel, which is thus broken
in pieces. One of the relations of the bride, who
all this time remains veiled, lifts her from her
palfry, and, carrying her into the reception room,
places her on a seat. In this room are entertained
all the female friends of the parties; the married
and unmarried being distinguished from each
other by their head-dress: that of the matron
consisting of an ornament of silver gilt, while the
virgins wear a turban of white muslin, sometimes
ornamented with printed flowers.

The husband then proceeds to conduct his relations and friends into another reception room, in a different part of the building. These ceremonies are repeated every day during a whole week; the entire assembly, who, not unfrequently, amount to five or six hundred individuals, going every day to the house of the bridegroom, where they eat, drink, and make merry. Sometimes they vary their amusements by proceeding outside the town, where they erect tents, and make a *fête champêtre;* the sexes remaining separate during the whole of the ceremonial. The expense of this, as well as of all the other preparations, is borne exclusively by the bridegroom and his friends. The tent of the bride is usually of a light-blue colour. Singing, dancing, and feasting occupy the whole time till the seventh day, when every one separates to his respective home, leaving the happy pair to the undisturbed enjoyment of their felicity. Matrimonial squabbles are almost unknown; and the love so solemnly plighted at the altar abides, through good and evil, as long as life endures.

Seven days, too, is the period during which they mourn the loss of a relation or friend. Formerly, a person dying in the morning was buried at mid-day. This practice has, however, been altered, in consequence of a discovery that individuals had been interred alive, and the period has been extended to twenty hours. During the above-mentioned seven days, nothing is heard but the voice of sorrow and lamentation; every day the friends and relatives of the departed repair to his grave, watering it with their tears, and making the air resound with their wailings. In addition to these, mourners are hired, who sing songs of lamentation, and put on the semblance of grief. During forty days the tomb is visited twice a week, and also upon every Sunday, for the space of a year, for the purpose of prayer.

Among no classes of mortals is filial affection more strikingly apparent than in these Christian communities; in nearly all cases the father remains with his children until his death, when he is replaced by his eldest son, to whom a like respect is immediately accorded.

Near Telkef, in the hollow formed by three hills whose lower portions unite at this spot, there is a remarkable chasm, supposed to have been caused by a thunder-bolt; it is not more than twenty feet deep, but it is impossible to ascertain how far the rent extends in a lateral direction, its sides having never been seen by mortal man. In winter it becomes a lake; but during the intense heat of summer it is left dry. The inhabitants consider it to be infested by reptiles of hideous form, and therefore hold it in great dread. A woman, I remember, once fell into this pit, and was with difficulty extricated by ropes.

Not long since an event took place in this town, which is by the inhabitants regarded, and not without strong grounds, as a miracle, not inferior to some recorded in Scripture. The lime, of which the powerful cement I have spoken of is manufactured, is obtained from the coarse marble of the adjoining mountains, by burning it in a vast furnace, fed with hay, the only fuel in this part of Asia. A poor man, noted for his sincere belief in the doctrines of Christianity, as well as for his blameless and virtuous life, was one day employed in tending one of those huge furnaces, on the top of which he had taken his post when, without the slightest warning, the roof which intervened between the poor Christian and the burning mass beneath, gave way with a loud crash, carrying him with it, apparently into the very heart of the living fire.

Of course no one imagined that he had not fallen
an immediate sacrifice to the burning lime; a
number of men were shortly after set to work, to
remove the loose stones which had fallen into the
hollow chamber of the furnace. For two days were
they engaged in this labour, not even expecting to
find the charred bones of their comrade. When,
however, they had well nigh completed their labour,
they were struck dumb with amazement at hearing
the voice of their lost companion. They instantly
redoubled their efforts, for hope had taken the
place of despair; the sounds of their axes and
spades were as thick hail. In a few minutes more
they had the happiness to behold their friend, who
had been preserved by a miracle, the falling stones
having taken the form of an arch, thus protecting
him from the flames, and preventing his immediate
suffocation. Like Sidrach, Misach, and Abdenago,
who preferred to suffer death by the furnace
of burning fire, rather than worship the golden
statue, the poor man walked alive from the
blackened heap.

Great was the wonder of his deliverers, who, like
the conscience-stricken idolator suddenly awakened
to a lively faith, exclaimed with Nabuchodonoso,

" Blessed be the God of them (to wit, of Sidrach, Misach, and Abdenago,) who hath sent his angel, and delivered his servants that believed in him."

The inhabitants of Telkef keep harmless snakes in their houses, and regard them with a veneration almost equal to that paid by the Romans to their household deities.

During our stay at Telkef we often indulged in the sport of catching quails, a favourite pastime here, where they are found in incredible numbers. The party proceed to the desert, where a temporary hut is erected, capable of holding two or three persons. From this cabin issue cords, attached to which is a large net of great length, which, as well as the cord connected with it, is entirely concealed by hay and corn strewed over it. The preparations being made, the party conceal themselves in the hut, holding in their hands the cords connected with the net, which is soon covered by myriads of the birds, all eager for food, and unconscious of their danger. When a sufficient number are collected the party suddenly pull the cords, by which the net closes, and makes prisoners of all that were perched upon it. I have frequently seen not fewer than a thousand of the heads of these

unhappy little creatures, trying to force themselves
through the meshes of the net, and screaming for
liberty in tones that went to my very heart.   We
frequently carried off several mule and ass loads,
the produce of our day's sport.

Upon one occasion, I remember, when we were
returning from a day's amusement of this kind,
laden with our booty, we were set upon by a party
of vagabond Arabs, who, seeing so small a party,
thought they might with safety venture to attack
us.   We were so few, that resistance would have
been the excess of madness and folly; we had,
therefore, no choice but to submit.   We were soon
rifled of every thing, quails, horses, mules and asses.
At this juncture, one of my brothers ran up to an
eminence, from which he could be seen by the
townspeople of Telkef, and taking up a quantity
of sand cast it into the air.   This well-known
signal was happily discerned by our friends, who,
without losing a moment, saddled their horses,
and, armed to the teeth, galloped to our rescue.
Our despoilers, who had, in the meantime, deemed
it prudent to quit the field, were hotly pursued by
our friends, who soon returned, having succeeded
in recapturing all we had lost, besides giving the

cowardly marauders a sound thrashing. We insisted on presenting our friends and deliverers with the greater portion of our game, and what remained was distributed to the poor.

If I have dwelt at some length on the manners, customs, and general characteristics of the inhabitants of this small town, my simple desire has been to secure for the Asiatic professors of our holy religion in general, that esteem, respect, and sympathy, from their European brethren in Christ, to which their manifold virtues entitle them; and I consider that I could accomplish this in no way so efficiently, as by detailing, with all candour and truth, the feelings and habits of a community amongst whom I passed several years of my life.

Since that time it has been my lot to be thrown amongst other communities of Oriental Christians; and I think I may fearlessly assert, that in no social point do they differ from those whom I have here attempted to describe. I am anxious to rescue them from the imputations I have heard cast upon them, of intolerant bigotry, and fanatical cruelty.

Far be it from me to desire to place my poor oppressed Christian fellow-countrymen upon a level with their enlightened European brethren, in any thing that appertains to the refinements of physical existence, or skill in polemical controversy. To these we make no pretensions. We are humbled in the dust. "Our inheritance is turned to aliens; our houses to strangers. We are become orphans, without a father—our mothers are as widows. We have drunk our water for money: we have bought our wood. We were dragged by the necks; we were weary, and no rest was given us." Our mighty cities, many leagues in length, with their swarming millions, their thousand lofty towers, and their high walls, are desolate and waste, the home of the jackall and the hyæna. Only the growl of the tiger, or the yell of the still fiercer Wahābi, pouncing on the unwary traveller, is now heard, where the soft strains of timbrel and harp once lulled the debauched senses of princes, who forgot their God.

I shall, I hope, be pardoned if—having been born and educated in a society in which the rude and primitive virtues of honesty, sincerity, and devotedness to the will of God, stand paramount in the estimation of its members—I use my humble endeavours to vindicate the characters of men who, though occasionally exposed to rapine and bloodshed, and surrounded by some who account the life of a fellow-creature of no more value than that of the brute which perisheth, can nevertheless, preserve the Christian feeling of compassion for their fellow-men.

CHAPTER V.

A Caravan—An Adventure with Kurd Robbers—Dreadful
Slaughter and Sufferings—Alkoush—Vast Christian Monastery—Severe Penance—Persecution of Christians—Journey
to Bagdad.

From Telkef we returned to Mosul ; whence
we set out, shortly after, for Alkoush, a small
town to the north of Mosul, where the prophet
Nahum is buried. As the road is not unfrequently
infested by some of the predatory hordes that
swarm in Mesopotamia, we thought it a necessary
precaution to seek out others who were going in
the same direction, for the sake of mutual security.
It was not long before we learned that a caravan,
with about a hundred persons, was on the point of
starting for the place of our destination. We
eagerly availed ourselves of the opportunity ; and
my mother, one of my brothers, and myself, at-

tended by only one servant, forthwith proceeded to join the party.

As we had a journey of twelve hours to perform, we started at sun-rise. We proceeded pleasantly onward the greater part of the day, and being favoured with extremely fine weather, our party were all in the highest spirits, passing in our way Telkef, Batmai, and several other villages, all consisting of houses substantially built of stone, in the manner which I have already described.

Evening was now drawing on apace. We had journeyed till we were within about four leagues of Alkoush, and were approaching the foot of a chain of mountains, notorious as the scene of many a pillage. The sun had gone down, and the deep shade thrown by the huge dark masses which flanked the gorge into which we were now about to enter, prevented us from seeing whether our passage was likely to be interrupted. My brother, therefore, offered to ride to the top of an eminence a little way in advance, whence he could see for some distance around, and bring us intelligence of the result. This offer was eagerly accepted by the whole caravan, whose hilarity had in some degree subsided, and given place to doubt and

apprehension.   My brother immediately set spurs
to his horse, and in a twinkling disappeared round
the shoulder of the mountain : for he was as gallant
a youth as ever put foot into stirrup.

We all awaited his return in breathless anxiety ;
but we waited long in vain.   At length, when we
began to fear that some accident must have befallen him, we were surprised by seeing him again
turn the side of the mountain, having on each side
of him a horseman, whom we discovered, by their
long beards and hair, and their ferocious aspect,
to be Kurds, from the neighbouring mountains of
Sinjar, the most lawless desperadoes on the face of
the earth.

" Who are these !" exclaimed my mother, in an
agony of affright.   " Are you bringing a band of
robbers to despoil and murder us ?"   All further
questions were put an end to by the arrival of a
large body of mounted bandits, who came gallop-
ing down the hill like a cloud of locusts.   It was
now too evident that we were in the hands of
robbers, who, to all appearance, far outnumbered
our small band.

My brother, and those who had the stoutest
hearts, immediately prepared for resistance, and,

with dauntless resolution, determined rather to
perish than suffer those they held most dear to
become the prey of lawless rapine and violence.
My mother was half dead with terror. She wept,
she screamed, and on her knees implored my
brother to give up all, rather than rush on certain
destruction. He was, however, deaf to all her
entreaties. His courage was roused. He was determined to yield nothing. As for myself, I
cannot say that I greatly participated in the alarm
felt by my mother, but was rather struck with the
noble daring of my brother; for my mind was cast
in a masculine mould, nor was I haunted by fears
for my own personal safety. "What!" exclaimed
I to my mother, "would you have your son act the
part of a coward, by tamely submitting, with arms
in his hands? If you cannot inspire them with
courage, do not weaken their resolution by your
womanly fears. Fear not—oh, my mother—God
will not desert the righteous!"

The parties by this time were ranged opposite
to each other; the Kurds, with their long lances
in their hands, reining in their pawing steeds, who,
as well as their lawless riders, seemed eager for the
fight, and impatient of all delay.

"Your property or your heads!" exclaimed the chief; which was answered by words of defiance from my brother. Without further parley, on rushed the marauding band with impetuous violence, uttering horrid yells and imprecations, the bright points of their lances glittering in the air. They were met as resolutely by our small band, and almost in the twinkling of an eye, the *melée* became fierce and general. My mother and I stood at the foot of the mountain, waiting with trembling hearts the issue of the desperate conflict.

Never, as long as I live, shall I forget the dreadful scene. The savage yells of the Kurds, thirsting for blood; the clattering and snorting of the horses—betokening a deadly struggle; the shouts of the living, the groans of the dying, and the piercing shrieks of my mother, called for the exercise of all the fortitude I could summon to my aid. On both sides the combatants were falling; some struck down by a slight wound, and others writhing and gasping in the agonies of death. Though covered with wounds, my brother still continued the unequal contest, until, overpowered by numbers, and fainting from loss of blood, he was compelled to submit, and the rest of the party followed his example.

The victors immediately began an indiscriminate and relentless pillage, sparing neither age nor sex in their unmeasured rapacity. They seized upon everything we had, horses, camels, and baggage; and concluded by stripping all who had survived the slaughter, of everything they had on. It was only by employing the most abject entreaties that I, at length, prevailed upon them to leave my mother, myself, and two ladies who accompanied us, a single under garment to cover our nakedness.

At length, sated with bloodshed and plunder, the Kurds quitted the field, having killed fifteen of our party, and wounded nearly all who remained, some of them severely; amongst whom was my dear heroic brother, who lay faint and almost senseless from loss of blood. Neither could the enemy have carried off a less number of killed and wounded on their side; for our party, though small, fought like lions. During the whole of this fearful contest, which lasted about three quarters of an hour, I never ceased to address words of encouragement to our valiant little band.

Here, then, were we left, four leagues from the place of our destination, despoiled of everything we had, without camels, without horses, without any means of conveyance, and nearly our whole party so badly wounded as to be almost incapable of proceeding on foot; the men stripped naked, and we with nothing on but our chemises. What was left us but to lie down and die? How could we hope to traverse with our bare feet the rough and stony mountain path that led to Alkoush?

We resolved, however, to make the effort, and summoning up all our resolution, we left the blood-stained spot, and commenced ascending the hill before us. My mother, though not wounded, was so entirely deserted by her faculties, that she had not the power to walk, and I was obliged to carry her on my back; for my brother's wounds prevented him from rendering us any assistance. Indeed, poor fellow, he needed assistance as much as any of us.

At length, after a painful journey of many hours, during which we were constantly compelled to halt—I, from the fatigue of carrying my burthen, and my brother, from the agony and exhaustion occasioned by his wounds—we managed to reach a

village within a short distance of Alkoush, where
we were most hospitably treated by its chief, to
whom my father was well known. He not only
caused my brother's wounds to be bound up, but
fed and supplied us with clothing. Amongst all
the effects of which I was plundered by the
Kurds, the article I most regretted the loss of
was a book of prayers, on which I set a high
value.

At this village we were detained three days, in
consequence of my brother's wounds, which were
so severe as to prevent his being removed. At the
expiration of that time, when, by our unremitting
attentions, aided by his own excellent constitution,
he was sufficiently recovered to proceed, we wrote
to an aunt of mine, living at Alkoush, who forthwith sent her son with horses for us; upon which
we took leave of our host, who had so kindly
administered to our necessities whilst we were
under his hospitable roof. We were not long in
reaching the place of our destination, where we
remained a month, until my brother was completely cured of his wounds.

Alkoush is situated at the foot of a lofty mountain, on each side of which arises a mountain of

lesser height. About half an hour from it stands
a convent called Deir Rabban Hormuz, placed on
the summit of a very high mountain, the view
from which is grand and imposing; it is now
inhabited by learned men and hermits. It contains
twelve churches, thirty-six courts, and an incal-
culable number of chambers. Its catacombs extend
almost to Alkoush, so vast are its dimensions.
The gates of the *sanctum sanctorum* in the great
church, which are ten paces wide, are all of ivory,
elaborately sculptured into an endless variety of
devices.

In this castle, or monastery, are found men skilled
in all branches of learning and science. Greatly
do those travellers deceive themselves, who imagine
that Arabia contains only marauding idolaters
and unenlightened Christians. Among the re-
cluses of the monastery Deir Rabban Hormuz are to
be found men who, in the above respects, would
not disgrace any of the schools of Europe. Here
are educated missionaries for the propagation of the
Christian faith throughout the East. Many a time
has the castle been attacked by the lawless bands
of Kurds, ever hovering about these mountain
districts, who have massacred numbers of its in-

mates, despoiling them of all they could lay hands on, and carrying off camel-loads of treasure. Scarcely less often have they been subjected to the rapacity of the neighbouring Pashas, in the employment of the government, who have robbed the sanctuary and scattered its peaceful inhabitants. After a brief interval they have, however, always succeeded in again obtaining a footing on their beloved mountain, where, by strict frugality, they have soon acquired sufficient wealth to prosecute the object of their existence, the propagation of the faith.

My father had a great share in upholding this religious institute, and always, to the utmost extent of his means, supported it through good and through evil; for, in addition to his pious zeal, he was always most anxious to promote the diffusion of knowledge and science in the East, where once shone the light, which shed its rays over the rest of the world, but now, alas! sunk in ignorance and barbarism. From this reproach he thirsted to rescue the Asiatic name, and spared no exertions to accomplish so noble an object.

Around the monastery are lands which are cultivated, and yield abundantly; the produce of which, after supplying its inhabitants, is distributed to the surrounding poor. There is scarcely an uncultivated patch of ground to be seen around the bottom of the mountain, where alone cultivation is practicable.

All around the tomb of the prophet Nahum, who was born at Alkoush, the Jews have built a synagogue, where they perform their religious rites, in conformity with the law ordained by Moses. My curiosity once tempted me to visit this synagogue during divine service; for doing which, I remember, I incurred the severe displeasure of my father. These Jews are far more strict in their observances than those of Europe, and would rather suffer death than consent to shave their beards.

The Christians of this town are sedulous in their pious exercises, occupy themselves much in the study of sacred books, and acknowledge the Pope to be the head of the Church. Twenty days before Lent they perform their penance in strict conformity with that practised by the ancient inhabitants of Nineveh to avert the wrath of God; fasting rigidly, and clothed in sackcloth, with ashes on their heads, for three days, a practice prevailing throughout Assyria. This observance, which I do not remember to have seen practiced elsewhere, has prevailed from generation to generation ever since the fall of Nineveh.

The inhabitants of Alkoush are a fine race, tall and well built, with complexions fairer than those of the inhabitants of the plain. The women wear a singular head-dress, having an ornament mostly of silver-gilt, extending considerably above the head, in a curved form, which is attached by a red ribbon. The men wear the red tarboosh, descending to the waist behind.

My brother being sufficiently recovered from his wounds to be capable of undergoing the journey, we set out on our return to Mosul; where we were doomed to trials far more severe than those we had suffered at the hands of the Kurdish bandits.

As the existing Christian church in Telkef was found wholly inadequate to contain the Christian population of that place, my grandfather was most anxious to obtain permission from the Pasha of the district to build one, of dimensions more suitable to the wants of the community. At length, after much negotiation, he succeeded in tranquillizing the conscience of the Mussulman by a present of immense value, and obtained permission to build a church within certain limits, beyond which he was strictly forbidden to encroach.

My grandfather set about his pious work with so much alacrity, that at the end of twenty days an edifice was completed, fully capable of accommodating all the Christian inhabitants. The old church and the new were enclosed within one wall, round the inside of which were arranged dwelling-places for the officiating priests. In the Christian churches of the East no layman is suffered to encroach upon the sacred precincts of the altar. The high altar is separated from the body of the church, above the flooring of which it is raised three steps, by a partition, having a door in the centre; and if a lay stranger is permitted to enter, he is always carried in the arms of two priests.

By some misapprehension, the architect whom my grandfather had employed to build the church, exceeded the limits prescribed by the Pasha by not more than three feet; an error which would, perhaps, have escaped observation, had it not been for a fanatical Turk, who lost no opportunity of inflicting injury on his Christian fellow subjects;

by which he hoped, not only to render himself
acceptable to the then authorities, ever glad of an
opportunity not only of gratifying their rapacity,
but also of acquiring a character for great sanctity
amongst men as misguided as himself.

This man, who was ever on the watch to detect
Christians in stepping beyond the laws, repaired to
the Pasha, and accused my grandfather of having
treated his injunctions with contempt. An inquiry was thereupon instituted, measurements were
made, and my grandfather summarily convicted of
the crime alleged against him.

The result may be readily anticipated. A fanatical mania spread like wildfire through the town.
The Mahometans assembled in hordes, and straightway proceeded, amidst shouts and imprecations,
to demolish the sacred building, on which my
grandfather had so recently expended such a vast
sum of money. Twenty days were they occupied
in the work of destruction; so substantially was it
built: but nothing could resist their headlong fury.
They were like a horde of ravenous wolves; for
they have a saying, "that every Christian church
is a burden upon the head of Mahomet;" every
additional foot, therefore, they considered an aug-

mentation of the heavy load already pressing upon
the forehead of the holy prophet.

My grandfather and father, together with his
brothers and sons, were, with many of the influential
Christians of the place, cast into prison; where
they were loaded with heavy chains, and subjected
every day to the torture of the bastinado.

The alternative was offered them of embracing the
faith of Islam or of suffering a painful and ignominious death. Undismayed by the dread of the cruel
fate, which their knowledge of Turkish barbarity
had taught them to expect, one and all, calmly but
resolutely, refused to renounce the faith in which
they had been born and educated, and in which,
by the blessing of the Almighty, they determined
to die, though their last agonies should, by all the
refinements of torture, be protracted to the last
extremity.

As for myself, I exulted at the prospect of martyrdom, which I fondly hoped to be permitted to
share with my dearly beloved parents. Not a
sigh, not a lamentation, escaped my lips. My
heart was full to overflowing with holy fervour
and pious hope. I assembled my friends around
me, and made them join with me in songs of

praise and thanksgiving. I went about as though clad for a festival, crying aloud, " This day shall I behold the face of the Lord. What are the treasures of this world? They are as chaff, which the wind separates from the ear, and scattereth in the desert. Let us, then, rather imitate the blessed martyrs, and this day purchase the eternal treasures of heaven with our blood."

But I was doomed to disappointment. The lust of gold prevailed in the heart of the tyrannical oppressor over his thirst for blood. My grandfather and father and my uncles, together with their relations and adherents, were at length released from the barbarous treatment to which they had been subjected, upon payment of a sum nearly equivalent to ruin, and which compelled my father to part with land, mills, manufactories, camels, horses, houses, gold, silver, and jewels—in short, with nearly all he possessed, until he was reduced from a state of opulence to one of comparative beggary.

Nothing daunted by these cruel reverses, my father had no sooner recovered from the wounds inflicted on him by the merciless bastinading to which he had been subjected, than, putting his trust in God, he set out with a firm reliance upon his heavenly mercy and justice, for Bagdad, accompanied by his family. Having reached that city, and placed my mother and myself in a house which belonged to him at a short distance from that in which I had passed the happy days of my childhood, he set out for Bassorah, where he had relations, in the hope of repairing, by unremitting industry and perseverance, his shattered fortune.

CHAPTER VI.

The Tower of Babel—Ancient Babylon—Return to Mosul—
A Life of Solitude—Life in the East—An Arabian Steed—
Festival — Frightful Persecution and Sufferings — Fearful
Pestilence—Return to Bagdad.

At the end of two years, during which it had
pleased Providence to crown his unceasing efforts
with success, my father resolved to return once
more to Mosul, for the purpose of re-establishing
his manufactories, again acquiring his lost possessions, and once more rallying round him the
Christian community, of which he had for so long a
time been considered the head. Nor was it without a reasonable hope of success that he determined
to undertake the task ; for he had been fortunate
in commerce at Bassorah, and had contrived, by
dint of frugality, to lay by a considerable sum of
money.

During our stay near Bagdad I made more than once an excursion to the ruins of the Tower of Babel. They were situated about a day's journey from our house, on the road to Hillah, where that ancient Babylon, "glorious among kingdoms, the famous pride of the Chaldeans," the city so great among the nations of the earth, once stood. These ruins are supposed by the inhabitants of the country to be the abode of evil spirits, the dwelling place of devils; and I must confess, that I was myself so far infected with the feeling, as to provide myself with some relic whenever I ventured there.

I was sixteen years old when we returned to Mosul, the scene of our former calamities. We had not long been there when my father began once more to erect mills, and establish manufactories in the adjacent town of Telkef. For some years we led a life of great tranquillity and happiness, receiving visits and attentions from all classes of persons, and amongst others from many chiefs of the Bedouin and Kurd wandering tribes, who frequently came to see us, and were on terms of great intimacy with my father. We all resided, my father with his family and also my uncles, in one spacious mansion; altogether we were not fewer than forty souls, including servants. The ground, covered by the house in which we lived, together with its courts, could not, I am certain, have been less than the space covered by the Louvre at Paris.

Preferring a life of solitude, I had a chamber fitted up for myself at the top of the house, on the terrace, where I had my meals brought to me daily. I was thus enabled to devote my whole time to study, prayer, and devout meditation. The only visitors I received were some ladies residing in the neighbourhood, who fully sympathized with me in my religious fervour. I lived sparingly, and slept but little. Often have I, at midnight, gone forth, when every sound was hushed, and a solemn silence reigned, only broken at intervals by the melancholy cry of the jackal or the howl of the wolf; the mountain tops of the distant range lighted up by the peaceful moon, by whose rays I would for hours read my favourite sacred writings. I would sometimes remain for three hours upon my knees, during which I would repeat many of the psalms: for at this time I had the whole of them by heart.

In the morning I rose betimes, and repaired to

the church, which was at the distance of half an
hour's walk from our house.   I frequently arrived
there an hour before the opening of the gates,
which took place at seven o'clock.   In the depth
of winter, which in this part of Asia is most severe,
I have often remained there until the gates should
be opened, kneeling on the threshold, till the cold
has almost paralyzed my limbs.   I remember once
remaining in this attitude during a hail storm, so
tremendous that the oldest inhabitant of the place
had never witnessed the like.   Some of the hail-
stones were of the size of walnuts, by the fall of
which more birds were killed than had ever before
been remembered.

Upon another occasion I had the misfortune to
be bitten by a scorpion, in the summer, while
waiting for the opening of the church gates.
Though I was suffering intense pain I persisted in
my devotions; at length I was carried into a
chamber adjoining the church, where caustic was
applied to the wound.   For the space of twenty-
four hours I endured excruciating torment; and
it was, indeed, a miracle that I escaped death.
My parents being informed of what had taken
place, had me forthwith conveyed home.

At this distance of time when I look back upon these events, and reflect on the torture which I then voluntarily, I may say cheerfully, endured, I can hardly believe in my own identity. Alas! how many years of sorrow have I passed since that period, when I fondly hoped that my days would be even as the eagle's flight. I had but tasted that cup of bitterness which I appear doomed to drain to its very dregs! Often have I been tempted to cry out with the Psalmist—"Lord why castest thou off my prayers? why turnest thou away thy face from me? I am poor and in labours from my youth, and being exalted have been humbled and troubled. Friend and neighbour thou hast put far from me, and my acquaintance, because of misery."

These few years were among the happiest of my life. Blessed with all that this world can give worthy of acceptance; happy in the love of the tenderest of parents, who now, unmolested in the prosecution of his plans for the welfare of his family, and the good of his fellow-men, spent all the time he could spare from the duties of his active life, in the bosom of his family, I lived in friendly intercourse with those of my friends who sympathized with me in my religious affections, and in

the enjoyment of full leisure for prayer and meditation.

Not a day passed on which I did not visit the
poor and the sick of the neighbourhood; admi-
nistering, to the best of my humble ability, temporal relief and spiritual consolation.   Three times
in the day I regularly attended our beautiful
church service ; which is of so impressive a character, that I once remember seeing even an
European gentleman, who was on a visit to us, and
had accompanied us to the recitation of the divine
office, moved to tears by its touching solemnity.
Throughout all Assyria and Chaldea, in Christian
churches, it is performed in the following manner.

The congregation is separated into two equal
parts; each of which, in the church I was in the
habit of attending, seldom numbered fewer than
a hundred.   In the front of each division are the
officiating priests.   Before each chorus, is to be
seen a huge book, placed by two men on a stand,
it being too heavy to be lifted by one.   The letters
are an inch in length.   From these books the congregation proceed to sing portions of the Psalms
of David and the Canticles; their voices trembling
with pious extacy.   Our European friend assured

us, that though he had travelled much, and been
present at religious ceremonies, in nearly every
part of the globe, he had never in his life witnessed solemnities, so calculated to inspire religious
thoughts, and fill the heart with pious aspirations.
In summer, these ceremonies are performed in the
open court.

These occupations were occasionally relieved by
a ride into the surrounding country, with my
brothers, when spring clothed the fields with the
many-hued luxuriance of Asiatic verdure; and
when the ground was sparkling with flowers of
every colour, and the vast fields of unripe corn,
agitated by the gentle breezes, looked like a
boundless sea of verdure, stretching far beyond
the ken of mortal vision.

We usually selected the banks of the Tigris, or
one of its tributaries, for the scene of our excursions. One day, I remember, when, in company
with my brother and uncle, I was riding on the
banks of the Haousera, which is the Chaldean
name for a branch of the Tigris, on which were
erected many of my father's mills. My brother
happened to be mounted on a mare of rare price,
and of the purest Arab blood, of the breed e.

kaheilani, which belonged to my father, and upon
which he set a high value. Her neck was as the
rainbow ; her eyes were like a living coal ; her mane
and tail like the drooping willow ; her feet were
as the stag's ; and her gallop was as the eagle's
flight. Many Bedouin chiefs had endeavoured to
possess themselves of this mare, and all declared
her matchless. She was fed principally on rice
and bread ; and was so docile and intelligent, that
little children often laid on the ground and played
with her hoofs, without receiving any injury.

My brother, while we were riding along the
bank of this river, was seized with the inclination
to swim the mare in the stream which flowed
beneath. She fearlessly plunged in : for had
it been the strait of Bab el Mandel, the high
couraged animal would not have flinched. The
stream was more rapid than my brother had looked
for. After many fruitless attempts to extricate
the poor creature, it became a question whether
he should leave the mare to her fate, or perish
with her ; for she had been so long in the
water that she had lost all power of making any
efforts for her own preservation. At length he
threw himself off her back, and by dint of great

exertion, stemmed the current and reached the shore.

Thus perished one of the finest and most beautiful steeds ever bred in Arabia; and for which my father might have received almost any price he chose to demand. Far, however, from heaping reproaches on the head of his imprudent son, who had been the cause of this irreparable loss, he bore this calamity, as he had already done others of far higher moment, with Christian forbearance and resignation. The body of the mare was afterwards recovered, and her heart was buried in a spot at the foot of a mountain.

We had now, for some years, led a life of uninterrupted felicity; when my father resolved to give an entertainment to his relatives and friends, in the open air, at a charming spot, not far from Mosul, on the banks of the Tigris. This was one of the ways in which he greatly loved to show his hospitality; and upon this occasion, as on many similar ones, he had invited, besides his numerous friends from Mosul and the neighbourhood, several of the chiefs of the Kurd and Bedouin tribes, with whom he always maintained an intimacy.

The day was extremely splendid. Nature was

decked in her holiday garments, for it was the
month of May. All around was smiling. Adversity seemed to have taken leave of us for ever.
My father had, once more, become wealthy.
Every thing seemed to promise him a dignified
and protracted old age, until the hour when it
should please Almighty God to gather him, full
of years, to his fathers.

Upon this spot we pitched our tents, one of
which was made in exact conformity with the
description given of Abraham's tent in the Bible,
and proceeded to spread out our entertainment.
Bullocks, lambs, and sheep had been slaughtered
upon the occasion, quails in abundance, preserved
by salting, fowls, and everything that could contribute to the enjoyment of our friends, were seen
amongst the viands. After making a substantial
meal we dispersed ourselves in various directions,
according as our fancy prompted. Beyond us
were the ruins of ancient Nineveh, telling nothing
of its grandeur, save its vastness. Mounds, extending miles and miles, as far almost as the eye
could reach, asserted the magnitude of the city
" of three days journey." I, with my companions,
wandered by the side of the river, chanting spiri-

tual songs, of which I had always an abundant store in my memory. In order to spare the religious prejudices of our Bedouin guests, I took care to be as far removed from them as possible during our pious pastime.

One of our shepherds, who had been converted to the Christian faith, was a Bedouin; and never was it my lot to meet any human being imbued with a more genuine Christian spirit. His conversion was owing to my own humble efforts; I therefore took great interest in his welfare. Nothing could exceed his resignation to the will of Providence. He never permitted himself to reckon with certainty on finding his wife and family alive on his return from tending the horses and sheep. His mind was ever prepared for any reverses that might befall him. Having once had the misfortune to lose his son, who fell a victim to the samiri of the Desert, a fiery blast, which frequently destroys those who encounter it, his only exclamation was, " the Lord gave, and the Lord hath taken away; as it hath pleased the Lord, so is it done : blessed be the name of the Lord !"

This was the happiest day of my life; my heart

was overflowing with gratitude and thanksgiving.
I had no wish or thought beyond that which it
had pleased Providence to bless *me* with at that
moment. All past cares and sorrows were forgotten, as things that had not been.

Seeing my father alone, at a short distance
from us, I quitted my companions and flew to his
side. He had never remained for so long a time
together, in the bosom of his family, as during
the last brief interval of tranquillity and peace.
I was never so happy as when I could enjoy his
society alone. Upon this occasion we wandered
for some hours on the banks of the Tigris;
our hearts swelling with gratitude to the Almighty
disposer of events for all his mercies.

"What happiness it is," I exclaimed, "thus
to pass our time in the uninterrupted society of
those who are dearer to us than life ! The voice
of our enemy is silent. He no longer takes
counsel for our destruction. If in this world of
care and misery, this vale of tears and sorrow, the
abode of mortal sickness and peril, such happiness
can be found, what may not the righteous expect
when they shall be called to receive their reward
in a better world; where there is no persecution,

neither shall the heart mourn the loss of kindred
and friends; where the enjoyment of happiness is
unembittered by the fear of losing it! Yet is not
all changeful and uncertain in this fleeting world,
and must not all joys and pleasures, like evil and
calamity, have an end? How happy, then, is he,
who, firm in faith, can quit alike the caresses of
prosperity and the frowns of adversity with the
calm smile of resignation! How blest is he whose
lofty soul can despise the storms of fate! Grant
us, O Lord God, deliverance from the robbers
and slayers of the Desert; shield us from the
pestilence; turn from us the wrath of tyrants;
pour the light of thy holy word into their hearts,
that they also may not, in the dread day of
reckoning, be cast into outer darkness, so that
we may end our days in thy service in holiness
and peace."

I besought my father that we might again
resort to this lovely spot together alone, and
again indulge in pious musings. He cheerfully
consented; but this was not to be. While my
fond parent was promising to himself and to me
many a happy hour of converse in this delightful
place, at that very moment a gulf was yawning

at our feet, which, ere long, was to close over all our worldly joys for ever.

Information had been carried to the ears of the Pasha, ever ready to entertain any charge against his Christian subjects, that treasure of immense value had been discovered by my father under the ruins of ancient Nineveh, and that he had appropriated it to his own use. In addition to this, he was accused of fomenting projects for the subversion of the Ottoman government and Islam.

Accusations more plausible could not well have been devised by men fully bent upon accomplishing his destruction. The time had not been long since my father had been reduced, by oppression and cruelty, to a state bordering upon beggary. He had again become wealthy ; his mills again reared their heads on the banks of the rapid Tigris, on its eddying journey to the great sea. His manufactories again found employment, and competence for those who would otherwise have been destitute. To his hospitable table the hungry and the naked were again admitted. The aged and the poor were again blessed with his bounty.

" How," exclaimed his enemies, " can these things be ?" The possibility of acquiring wealth by persevering industry, skill, spirit, and frugality, never entered the mind of his cruel and fanatical persecutors. A solution of the mystery must, however, in some way be found. And what solution so probable as that he, who dwelt amidst the ruins of ancient Nineveh, whose husbandmen daily worked amongst its mouldering remains, should have there discovered the wealth, which had made itself manifest in so many different ways?

A sincere, regular, legal investigation into the truth or falsehood of the charge was entirely out of the question. The bare suspicion was quite enough to justify extreme measures, more especially when the individual suspected happened to be a zealous Christian. With increasing means, my father was naturally enabled to give increased support to the Christian churches around him; and this just zeal in behalf of his own faith was easily perverted by designing men into a desire to undermine that of his rulers. But, whatever might be the impression on the minds of his persecutors, as to the truth of their accusation, there can be no

doubt as to the advantages they would derive from
the conviction of my father, namely, a second confiscation of his entire property.

Accordingly he was again cast into prison, together with his brothers, his former companions in
suffering.   Tortures, cruel and unceasing, were
resorted to, in order to force from him an acknow-
ledgment of his pretended crime, and a disclosure
as to the spot in which this pretended treasure was
hidden.   But all was in vain.   My poor father
had nothing to disclose.   The only result of all
their barbarity was to prove to his revilers with
what calm resignation a Christian, firm in his
faith, can endure the direst of sufferings.

But rapacity again prevailed. My beloved parent
was set at liberty ; the sentence of death having
been commuted to that of confiscation of his entire
possessions.   Broken down both in body and
spirit, covered with bruises and wounds, his feet a
shapeless mass of black, festering flesh, the effects
of the merciless blows of the bastinado, he was at
length turned out of his dungeon, and conveyed
to his home.   Oh, God! what a frightful change !
A short month since, and we were planning
projects of future happiness and harmless enjoy-

ments, during our happy walk on the banks of the Tigris.

Every thing that unremitting attention, aided by the care of the most skilful surgeons, could effect, was resorted to in vain. My dear parent sank gradually. Nature was exhausted. His sufferings had passed the limits of human endurance. From the first his case was pronounced hopeless. Three weeks after his release found him at his last gasp.

From the moment of his liberation, I never quitted his chamber. The awful moment now drew near. His soul, hovering over the brink of eternity, he called me to his bed-side. "Poor child," he said, in faultering accents, "what will become of thee? Who will protect thee from the enemies of thy race, who have slain thy parent, and driven thy kindred to herd with the wild beasts of the desert? Preserve in thy heart, my dear daughter, the lively faith already implanted there, and the fear of Almighty, and thou wilt have no need to dread the assaults of thy enemies. End thy days as thou hast begun them, a good Christian. God give thee patience in tribulation, and consolation in sorrow, until we again meet in that happy country where the humble followers of Christ need no longer dread the cruelty and oppression of unbelieving rulers."

He besought me not to put myself in peril, by journeying to distant countries, far from kindred and friends: for he well knew that I longed to behold the scenes where our Saviour had lived and taught. Having devoutly received the last sacraments, with all the other consolations of religion, he gave me his last benediction, and, with a countenance full of heroic composure and Christian resignation, he yielded up his soul to his Creator, with the words, "Into thy hands, O Lord, I commend my spirit!"

What language can express the horrors of that terrible moment! I had no tears to shed. The fountains of my soul were dried up: I expected my heart would burst. With the loss of my dear parent, my fortitude deserted me; I refused all consolation; night and day I gave myself up to weeping. I longed for death. I abandoned myself to sorrow, grief, and wailing. All this well nigh deprived me of reason. I fell sick of fever. God only knows how fervently I prayed it might prove mortal, that I might again behold the face of my beloved parent. It pleased Him to deny me that crown of martyrdom. I was doomed to live on, and to suffer.

This last persecution ended in the utter destruction of my family. One of my uncles expired, from the treatment he had received, shortly after my father. Another, who was Archbishop of Diarbekir, was bound on the back of a wild horse, which was then driven into the desert. Many days he was without food. At last, he succeeded in disengaging himself from his bonds, and, for fifteen days, subsisted on wild herbs, until at length he succeeded in reaching some place of safety. He was so fortunate as to reach a town; from whence he travelled much, with varying fortunes, over Persia, and other countries, and finally returned to Diarbekir, where he now resides.

My mother died of grief; surviving my father but a very short time.

The hand of Providence was heavy upon us. Nevertheless, my cup of bitterness was not yet full. Yet a little time, and a pestilence spread throughout the land, carrying off, in its ravages, ninety-five thousand souls in Mosul and its neighbourhood. Every one with whom I was connected

by blood in this, to me, ill-omened city, perished
by that plague—leaving me an orphan in the
wide world. I longed for death, but the destroying angel passed me by. I wandered about the
fields, scarcely knowing where I was, or what I
did. I passed on, heedless of surrounding objects ;
save when the sight of some well known spot lace-
rated my heart anew, by awakening it to a sense
of its bitter loss and mournful desolation.

Years and years after, upon seeing in a book at
the Asiatic Society in London, an engraving of
the bridge at Mosul, the tears gushed from my
eyes, as though my sorrow had been but a few
days old.

CHAPTER VII.

Journey to Bagdad—Serpents—I propose to establish an Institution for the Education of Women—A Story of the Wise
King—A Missionary—I visit a Bedouin Chief in his Encampment—Life in the Desert.

My father left me all that he had been able to
save from the wreck of his fortune, his ring, his
hanjar, and his watches; which, together with
some pearls and jewels of value and some Persian
shawls, were entrusted for security to the hands of
a bishop of his acquaintance who, seeing my forlorn
and destitute condition, kindly proposed to take me
with him to Bagdad. To this I assented, and we
left the ill-omened city, the scene of all my woes, a
few months after the frightful tragedy which had
torn from me all that rendered life desirable.

Our preparations being completed, we started
in company with a lady whom I knew, and a Kur-

dish jairiah, or slave, both of whom were Christians,
for Bagdad by the Tigris; having taken a kalak,
which is a raft made of inflated skins; on which
is erected a small cabin. In casting a look upon
the hated city, I could not help exclaiming, "Adieu,
thou abode of desolation, thou grave of all that I
ever loved upon earth! Farewell, accursed city,
blasted by the wrath of the Almighty for thy manifold sins and iniquities!" "Behold I come against
thee, saith the Lord of Hosts; and I will discover
thy shame to thy face, and will show thy nakedness to the nations, and thy shame to kingdoms.
And I will cast abominations upon thee, and
will disgrace thee, and will make an example of
thee. And it shall come to pass, that every one
that shall see thee shall flee from thee, and shall
say, Nineveh is laid waste; who shall bemoan thee?
whence shall I seek a comforter for thee?"

We occasionally quitted our kalak and walked
on the banks of the river, whenever we had to pass
a rapid, or when we were tempted to do so, by the
beauty of the spot, or the coolness of the air.

For a long time I remained silent, buried in
melancholy reflections on the past, and full of
dreary apprehensions for the future. In vain my

kind-hearted friend and protector endeavoured to draw me into conversation; in vain he tried every device he could think of, to rouse me from my lethargy. As we were passing the spot where streams of naphtha from the neighbouring mountain flowed into the Tigris, hoping thereby to draw my attention to the phenomenon, he flung lighted pieces of cloth into the water, which ignited the naphtha, and filled the majestic river with vivid seams of liquid fire. But all were of no avail. The iron had entered my soul. I had no eye for amusement, no ear for words of consolation. Even the offices of friendship had become irksome to me.

Thus did the first day pass over my head; during the whole of which I remained a prey to the bitterest reflections. We slept on board the kalak, and next morning I awoke with a mind more composed, and with a firmer resolution to submit without a murmur to the decrees of Divine Providence. During the night, I had implored the aid of the Almighty in my affliction; and that aid was not denied me.

We were now approaching that part of the Tigris where the navigation is both difficult and dangerous, from rocks in the bed of the stream,

which are almost high enough to be seen above the
water.   Accidents are frequent at this place, from
the bursting of the inflated skins of which the
kalak is composed, by coming in contact with
sharp angles of the rock.   On reaching this spot,
it is usual for all passengers, whether Christians or
Mahometans, to offer up prayers for their safety.

We took the precaution of landing just before
our vessel approached the scene of danger, con-
tinuing to walk by the river's side until we had
passed it.   And we had cause to congratulate ourselves on our prudence; for, on looking back, we
saw a child struggling in the water, which, in spite
of all the exertions that were made to save it, was
drowned before our eyes.   Like ourselves, its
parents were going down the stream in a kalak:
but unfortunately, relying on their skill to guide it
in safety, they did not leave it at the proper
moment.   The skin had burst, the raft had over-
turned, and the whole party, consisting of several
grown up persons, besides the child, were preci-
pitated into the water.   They were Bedouins,
and had all, both men and women, saved themselves by swimming; an exercise in which that
race, of both sexes, are remarkably expert.

We were told by the inhabitants of this spot, that serpents are frequently seen there of an enormous size and thickness, which are held in great dread from their ferocity. In making their attack, we were told that they draw themselves up into a perpendicular position, their body presenting the appearance of a huge club.

After a voyage of five days, we at length reached Bagdad. In early spring, when the snows on the northern mountains melt, and descend in torrents to the valleys, the stream of the Tigris is so rapid, that the journey from Mosul to Bagdad is performed in two days. As there is no accommodation of any kind for landing passengers, both men and women are carried on shore by parties who are naked, with the exception of a girdle. One of these men carrying in his arms a lady, had got within a few feet of the bank, when his foot slipped and he fell, together with his fair charge, into the water; an accident which occasioned a loud burst of laughter from those who had already landed. Such was the sympathy shown to this unfortunate lady, who was drenched from head to foot. It was many a day since a smile had been seen upon my countenance; I must, however, confess

that I could not repress one upon beholding the
ludicrous distress of the ill-starred lady; who be-
wailed her temporary distress as if it had been one
of the direst calamities that could have befallen
her.

On arriving at Bagdad, I went to the house of a
friend, and there took up my abode.

During the time that I remained at my friend's
house, a project entered my head, to which I forthwith directed all my energies; namely, to set on
foot an institution for the education of women.
This was a project which I had cherished from
early life.   I was not absolutely destitute of means.
With the little property that still remained to me,
together with the assistance of my friend, who was
wealthy, and whose co-operation I did not despair
of obtaining, I confidently hoped to be able to
carry my wishes into effect.

On first opening the subject to my protector, he
would not listen to it, but treated it as a visionary
scheme, which could have been only generated in
an over-sanguine and even a disordered imagination, and one which could not possibly lead to any
beneficial results.   I was not, however, to be easily
discouraged.   I endeavoured to raise his enthu-

siasm by setting before him, in as glowing colours as I possibly could, the glory that would result from rescuing the weaker sex amongst us from the inferiority, both moral and physical, in which they had hitherto continued, and the happiness that would attend those who should assist in raising them to that condition of usefulness for which they were designed by a beneficent Creator.

By what means, I asked, have they been reduced to this state? By ignorance. Who is it that has suffered them to remain in that ignorance? Who is it that has erected the dam which shuts out the streams of intelligence from their minds? Man. Man alone is the culprit. He first denies to women the means of attaining knowledge, and then avails himself of her ignorance, the consequence of his own neglect, as a justification for contemning his victim. Let it no longer be said that we imitate the fabled example of our infidel neighbours, in the treatment of our helpmates. Our religion teaches us better things. Let us not be Christians in name only. Where, I asked him, is it taught us by our church, that woman should be the slave of man? Was she not formed to be his companion, his solace, through all the changing

scenes of his earthly existence? On what pretence
then, does man assert his privilege to tyrannize
over our sex? Has not our sex more patient endurance, more tender attention than yours? Like
you, have we not an immortal soul? Are not the
sensibilities of woman as keen as, nay, keener than,
those of her lord and master? Has she not a heart
equally alive to gratitude; and a sense of wrong
as deep? Notwithstanding all this, she is often
treated as if she had neither a head nor a heart.

But our sex, it is said, is weak. True. I have,
however, known many a Bedouin woman, who, in
the management of a horse, or in throwing a
javelin, could vie with the best of you; and before
such I have seen many a man tremble. Neither
could I ever learn that this weakness obtained for
a female an exemption from the most laborious
and most fatiguing household duties. Her weakness is never thought of by her indolent lord:
who sits inertly by, smoking his ralioun, while his
wife is engaged in the not very gentle labour of
fixing his tent. If the Christian women of the east
are ignorant—if they are a prey to humiliating delu-
sions—it is because the cultivation of their minds
is neglected. It is this ignorance alone that makes

man the tyrant, and woman the sláve. Ignorance
is the bane: let us hasten to apply the antidote,—
religious education. In this way it was that I
reasoned with my friend. I then related to him
the following tale, which I had often heard my
dear father repeat.

" In old times, there was a nation, whose custom
it was to elect a king annually to reign over them.
To prevent jealousies and contentions, they never
fixed upon one of their own nation, but always
sought out some stranger, who might accidentally
be passing through their territories, and him they
placed on the throne. This they also did that
they might secure a sovereign free from the prejudices of their own people, and one who would
administer justice according to his own unbiassed
ideas of right and wrong.

" His year of office being expired, the king,
without any previous notice, was suddenly thrust
from the throne, and sent into a desert island,
with the loss of all his honours and wealth, and
deprived of the means of existence, to reflect at
leisure on the instability of human greatness.
Many had been taught this bitter lesson; when a
stranger happened to fall into their hands, in

whose mind was the salt of wisdom, and whose
cunning equalled that of the serpent.   Before this
stranger entered upon his kingly office, he took
care to ascertain, by diligent inquiries, the manner
in which the people, over whom he was called to
reign, usually treated their sovereigns, and on discovering their unceremonious way of cashiering
them, he said to himself, ' I am here as a sojourner.
I will therefore keep my mind fixed on that part
of my journey which lies beyond this my present
halting place.   Many are the temptations that will
beset me during my brief stay ; but, with the aid
of Providence, I will not suffer its allurements to
betray me into a forgetfulness of my permanent
interests, but will ever hold myself in readiness to
depart at the shortest warning.   The present
opportunity I will turn to advantage.   I will make
ample provision against a time of need; and will
thus frustrate the machinations of my cruel and
designing subjects.'

"Having taken this resolution, he accepted the
diadem, and during his year of office, administered
the laws in justice and mercy.   Never for a
moment did he lose sight of the rules he had laid
down for his conduct.   Though surrounded by

pleasures of every kind, he led a life of moderation and even austerity. If he ever found his firmness wavering, he said to himself, 'Remember, oh, my soul, thou art but upon a journey: thy haven of rest is afar off.'

"In the early part of his year's reign, he had the sagacity to discover the place of his future banishment. To this spot, therefore, he secretly conveyed abundance of cattle and treasures; and having so done, his heart was glad within him. 'Of a truth,' he said, 'I have kept the good resolution of my heart. I have not drunken with the drunkard; neither have I revelled with the reveller; in the midst of violent men, I have kept my hands from violence. Have I not now my reward?'"

When I had finished my story, I implored my kind friend and protector rather to imitate the example of the wise king, who, neglecting the pleasures and allurements of the present moment, made provision for that which was to come. "Life," I said to him, "is but a moment. Lay up, then, for yourself the riches of virtue and good works in this world; send them to that distant

land to which you know you must finally go, and
assuredly your soul shall not perish." In addition
to these arguments, I placed before him the condition of the weaker sex in Christian Europe, in
striking contrast with their position in the east.
Having, in the course of my studies, made myself
tolerably familiar with the Latin, Italian, French,
and Hindostanee, besides the Hebrew, Syriac,
Chaldaic, and other eastern languages, I was
enabled to avail myself of many authorities in
support of my proposition.

At last, I succeeded in convincing him of the
correctness of my views, and in inducing him to
lend his powerful aid towards the accomplishment
of my project, which, in the course of a few
months after my arrival at Bagdad, gave fair promise of a successful result.

Accordingly we took a spacious house, and
here we established our college, to which, in a
short time, flocked great numbers of every class
in society; for we made no distinction of rank.
Young girls, rich as well as poor, and even grown
up women of condition, desirous of obtaining
instruction, poured in incessantly. We taught

reading, writing, needle-work, and embroidery; and no pains were spared to inculcate the principles of the Catholic religion.

Thus tranquilly and successfully we proceeded, day after day adding to the number of our pupils ; actuated by no other ambition than that of making ourselves useful to our fellow-creatures, and, if possible, to redeem the female sex from the humiliating position in which they stood in our country. We sought not for celebrity, neither did we desire or expect interference ; when, suddenly, our labours were interrupted, our plans frustrated, and our institution itself was ultimately destroyed, by the officious intermeddling of a European missionary, who happened, at that time, to be residing at Bagdad.

This individual, who had obtained his appointment in the East by the influence of an illustrious personage, was of humble origin. His chief object was to amass wealth, of which he made a very foolish parade ; rivalling the Pasha himself in the breed of his horses, and in the richness and splendour of their trappings.

It is scarcely possible to conceive the injury, the deadly mischief, that has been done to the

true faith in the East, by missionaries, appointed
without any adequate investigation into the quali-
fications they possess for the high and sacred office
which they are called upon to fill. Too much
caution cannot be exercised in selecting men whose
duties are to inculcate the doctrines of meekness,
long-suffering, charity, and brotherly love, amongst
a people but too well accustomed, alas ! to behold
and feel the effects of opposite qualities in their
infidel rulers and fellow countrymen.

In so saying, I do but give the results of my
own experience, of not a few years, in the East,
the land of my birth; during which it has been
my lot to meet with numerous persons sent to
convert unbelievers, and confirm their Christian
brethren in the determination to hold fast the
true faith amidst stripes and bondage. None but
those who have lived amongst the persecuted
Christians of the East can have any conception
of the inestimable benefits which would result to
the cause of our holy religion, by the appointment of men fitted by vocation, education, and
genuine piety, for the high post of missionary;
neither can they form a just estimate of the
deadly blow inflicted on the righteous cause, by

the selection of men distinguished for qualities of an opposite description.

The individual to whom I have alluded, introduced himself into our humble, unpresuming establishment, with the avowed purpose of inculcating the principles of the Christian religion. He was received by us with open arms. He was welcomed as the special messenger of Christ; for such we of the East are ever disposed to view the European missionary—the hem of whose garments we were almost ready to kiss. To Europe we look for final deliverance from the yoke of the oppressor; and every Christian from Europe is therefore regarded and treated by us as a deliverer, and as such honoured far beyond his Asiatic brethren.

To this man, alas! I owed the frustration of my darling project. I might, perhaps, have stolen a march on the senseless and heedless Moslem, quaffing the fumes of fatalism on the musnud of security; but the conduct of the European completely baffled me, and once more made me an outcast on the world.

Having no power to resist, I at length yielded; and, weary of life, and thoroughly deceived in the estimate I had formed of mankind, I became desperate, and resolved to quit the crowded cities, where men, seemed only to congregate for the purpose of vilifying and injuring one another, and betake myself to the desert. I determined to go wherever my fancy or caprice led me; heedless of the consequences, so that I did but escape from the nest of hornets, into which my unlucky stars had cast me. " Amongst the wandering hordes of the desert," I said, " I shall at least meet with open friends and open enemies. I shall then meet no wolf in sheep's clothing, to fasten on his unsuspecting prey, who fed and protected him from the wintry blast. At least, I shall not fall by the dagger of him with whom I have broken my bread and eaten my salt."

Fully bent on carrying my purpose into execution, my heart filled with a loathing which had well nigh driven Christian charity from my breast, I addressed a letter to the chief of the Dryaah tribe, occupying the desert, in the neighbourhood of Babylon and Bagdad, with whom my father had been well acquainted, and who had many and many a time been our guest, during our sojourn at Bagdad, in happier days. Not in the least doubting that my letter would meet with a favour-

able reception, I made preparations for my immediate departure, and forthwith packed up all the
valuables I possessed, ready for my journey. I
was not disappointed. Shortly after I had dis-
patched my letter, the chief Dryaah Ebn Shalan,
sent his son and daughter for me, with camels to
carry my baggage, and his own favourite mare for
my especial use.

I was almost moved to tears by this kind attention to one who had nothing but thanks and good
wishes to offer in return; and that from a man
whom my late persecutors would have despised,
to the full extent that their fears would permit
them, as a lawless barbarian. Coming after so
many injuries, and so much sorrow, it seemed like
a ray from Heaven, to cheer me on my weary
pilgrimage. I set off with the son and daughter
of this kind-hearted Bedouin chief, as though I
had been going to my own parents; such was my
firm reliance on their hospitality, their inflexible
honour, and their adherence to their engagements;
and it was not long before we reached the encampment of the tribe, who had pitched their tents
upon a spot near the Euphrates, hard by the ruins
of ancient Babylon; which they had chosen on

account of its general fertility, and the abundance and excellent quality of the pasture.

Nothing could exceed the cordiality of my reception at the encampment. I had no sooner arrived at the tent of the chief Dryaah Ebn Shalan, than I was introduced to his wife and relatives, and treated with the highest distinction. The spectacle which presented itself to my sight, on approaching the encampment, was most imposing. On the right, and on the left, as far as the eye could reach, the vast plain was covered with tents; while countless flocks of sheep, camels and horses innumerable, were grazing on the pastures around. No mountain range, no tree, intervened to break the level surface of the plain which surrounded us on every side.

It was the month of May, and the fresh green of the spring grass was rendered doubly brilliant by the many-hued flowers which every where sprang up in profusion. The vast expanse of verdure was relieved by the beautifully winding Euphrates, whose gentle eddies, ever and anon catching the sun's rays as they emerged from the shadow of the hanging bank, flashed forth their joy, like the glad eye of early youth. It seemed made to be the abode of peace and innocence; and I appeared to myself to have been suddenly carried back to the age of the early patriarchs. " Where," I exclaimed, " shall the wounded spirit seek repose from its throes, if not here? Where shall the persecuted seek an asylum from the craft and subtlety of his persecutors, if not in this dwelling-place of peace; where nature lives in all her primeval simplicity; where the rude and sacrilegious hand of man has not been to mar and to destroy?"

The sense of liberty, the consciousness that I had emancipated myself from the thraldom of walled cities, which my sad experience led me to regard as the strongholds of cruelty and oppression, had something intoxicating in it. I had not felt such elasticity of spirits since the day I had spent with my poor father on the banks of the Tigris, when, little dreaming of the bitter woes in store for me, I gave myself up to the enjoyment of the moment, which I then, with a foolish confidence, considered to be the forerunner of many years of happiness.

The tent of the sheikh, or chief, was in the centre; it was about seventy feet in length, and made of black camel's hair, woven into a stout texture; it was divided into three parts, the centre being appropriated to the wife and her female attendants; the back, where also the provisions were kept, to the servants, who performed there the cooking and other household duties; and the front to the men, and to strangers who might happen to be on a visit to the chief; there also was situated the "rabka," or reception-room.

The customary compliments being over, we proceeded to make arrangements for my accommodation in the department allotted to the women. By means of putting up a curtain, I managed to secure for myself a sort of private apartment, which was particularly desirable, in order that I might not shock or offend my hostess, by the performance of certain religious duties, for which she might entertain an aversion.

Here I forthwith installed myself, together with my effects. I must, however, confess, that I could not contemplate, without a shudder, the idea of lying down to sleep at night upon the bare ground, with nothing but a carpet to protect me from the attacks of noxious reptiles, of which I always entertained the greatest dread. From infancy upwards

I had ever been accustomed to sleep on beds made
of palm leaves, resting on a frame constructed of
palm wood, and therefore I did not at first at all
relish the idea of changing this for a simple carpet.
Fortunately, there were no scorpions to be dreaded
here, otherwise I do not think, after what I had
already suffered from their bite, that any persuasion
could have induced me to trust myself on the
ground. In Bagdad it was, I remember, by no
means an uncommon thing, on rising in the morning, to find among the palm leaves one of these
poisonous reptiles, which had been impaled on one
of the sharp spines, in its endeavour to reach the
body of the individual sleeping above. Here, however, there were no fears on this score.

When we had completed our arrangements, my
kind entertainers immediately set about preparing
some refreshment. We all sat down to a repast,
consisting of dates fried in butter, eggs, and camel's
milk; to which primeval fare my keen appetite, the
result of a long ride, enabled me to do ample justice.

We were not long in despatching our meal, and
passed our time between that and dinner in taking
a walk upon the banks of the Euphrates, or " Nahr
al Fraat," as it is called by the inhabitants of the

country through which it flows. I never enjoyed
a stroll more; the sky was beautifully serene, the
air mild without being oppressive, and all nature
clad in her holiday suit. We came at every step
upon vast numbers of gazelles, which are found
here in an abundance almost incredible; never
did I see such immense flocks of them; during our
short walk I am sure I beheld thousands. Their
flesh is exceedingly good, and is held in high
esteem among the Bedouins, who constantly make
parties to hunt them; the flavour of their flesh is
not unlike that of a goose.

The sun had nearly reached the horizon, which
here presented precisely the same appearance as at
sea, when we returned to the tent of the sheikh,
where we found dinner prepared. The hour for
that meal was sunset. It was, therefore, not long
before we were all seated at the chief's hospitable
board. Our repast, it is true, was not distinguished
by any of the refinements of culinary science. There
was, however, no lack of good, substantial dishes;
and fastidious indeed must the individual have been
who could not have made a hearty meal out of the
dishes before him. Of roasted meats we had three
different sorts; sheep, lamb, and gazelles, of which

I am particularly fond. Besides these, there was a dish to which, during my abode with the Bedouins, I could never reconcile myself; and that was the leg of a camel roasted; though I daily saw them partake of it, apparently with infinite relish. To say the truth, these Arabs came to their dinner with appetites so sharpened by severe exercise, that I believe they would not have made wry faces even though it had been served up in an undressed state.

When the solid part of the meal had been disposed of, we were regaled with fruits of various descriptions. I myself had taken the precaution to bring with me a large supply of lemons, dates, figs, and almonds; besides cakes, dried fruits, and fruits preserved with sugar. So that I was enabled to contribute something to the feast.

The Bedouins eat with the hands alone; making use of neither knife, fork, nor spoon. "Allah," they say, "gave man a mouth and a pair of hands to be mutually serviceable to each other. Why, then, should we mock the Eternal Spirit by fashioning to ourselves strange implements of wood or metal? Shall the tooth despise the finger, or shall the finger forget the way to the tooth?

What fork is equal to nature's fork—the hand of man? Our ancestors," say they, "used no cunningly fashioned instruments. But did they, therefore, perish of hunger? Were their years not as the sands of the desert? In their bodies was the blood of health, and in their minds the salt of wisdom. Shall we then laugh at the beards of our fathers?"

Thus, with the means at hand of eating with forks of gold, they persist in eating with their fingers. I, who was less accustomed to such primitive usages, had brought with me a spoon; but, on learning the horror in which such contrivances were regarded by my hosts, I determined not to wound their feelings, and consequently conveyed the food into my mouth like themselves, though the consequence of my politeness was not unfrequently a scalded finger.

After dinner, coffee was introduced; for, unlike the Wahābis, whose rigid asceticism forbids them the use of this harmless stimulant, the Dryaahs do not forbid the enjoyment of it. This rejoiced me exceedingly; for I should have regretted the absence of the cup of coffee, to which I had been so long accustomed. There was, nevertheless, still a difficulty to be got over. The Dryaah tribe, abhor "the accursed weed," as they call tobacco, and prohibit the use of it.

I had so long been used to enjoy a nerghila after taking my coffee, that the prospect of losing the accustomed indulgence produced by no means a pleasing anticipation in my mind. I had brought all my apparatus with me, but was afraid to produce it, from the dread of shocking the scruples of my host and his friends. His considerate kindness relieved me, however, from my distress. When upon a visit to my father, he had observed that, in common with most others, I invariably took a nerghila after dinner. He, therefore, now insisted on my observing the custom, and kindly forbade the sacrifice which I was prepared to make to his own prejudices. The highest bred cavalier of civilized Europe could not have shown more genuine politeness.

Dinner being over, the company, according to custom, arranged themselves in a large circle, and proceeded, each in his turn, to relate anecdotes, which, in nearly every case, turned upon horses of rare breed, or of hair-breadth escapes, in desperate encounters with hostile tribes. These tales were relieved at intervals by singing, and one of the company, I remember, sang a song in a slow and plaintive measure, in such a manner as to prove that the wandering Arab tribes are not utterly devoid of musical talent. The air was extremely short, and sufficiently monotonous.

One of the stories pleased me much, from the sound morality which it tended to inculcate. It was, as far as my memory serves me, nearly as follows : —

" Once upon a time, there was a Bedouin chief called Rejal el Hamed, whose fortunate destiny made him the possessor of a mare of rare beauty and excellence, whose speed exceeded that of " el shemale" (the north-east wind) of the desert. Day after day was Rejal el Hamed beset by the most tempting offers from the chiefs of friendly tribes; but entreaty, gold, and silver, all were unavailing to induce him to part with his favourite steed.

" Now, there was another chief, called Faris el Aanta, who greatly desired to possess himself of this mare, whose fame so filled the land, that there

was no one to the north, to the south, to the east,
or to the west, who had not heard of her matchless
excellence.   Many were the offers sent by this
chief to Rejal el Hamed; which, however, produced no effect on the firm resolution which he
had taken to keep his mare, whatever temptation
might beset him.

"At length, the chief, Faris el Aanta, whose
longing, so far from being cured, had only
acquired increased keenness, from the oft-repeated
rejection of his offers, in a fit of despair, sent a
messenger to tender the whole of his possessions,—camels, flocks, all he had,—in exchange
for the much-prized mare.   But the chief was
inexorable ; for he thus reasoned with himself: —
'Faris el Aanta has camels; he has also horses
and many sheep : but have not others also camels,
and horses, and sheep?   And if he shall lose one
of these, will not he go to his neighbour and say,
Friend, I desire one of thy camels ; here is corn ;
take of it as much as thou wilt, so that I may take
with me one of thy camels.   But, in the following
year, the corn which he has given to his neighbour
shall be returned to him again by the fruitful earth.
But if I shall say to Faris el Aanta, take with thee

the mare, which is the sun-light of my heart, and give me in return what thou offerest, will the fat earth yield me another like her, whose speed is as the wind, and whose eye is like the living fire?'

"The chief, foiled in his attempt, and enraged at the indomitable obstinacy of his rival, determined to obtain by stratagem that which he had been unable to gain by open negociation, and the offer of all he possessed. He therefore resolved to disguise himself, and waylay the inexorable Rejal el Hamed as he should pass, and by cunningly devised pretences, obtain possession of his long wished-for treasure.

"Accordingly, having changed his garments, and stained his face with a herb, which communicated to it a ghastly aspect as of one suffering from some deadly disease, he lay down by the road side, where he knew well that the sheikh, Rejal el Hamed, was to pass, and patiently awaited his coming. He was not mistaken; for, before long, he espied his envied rival approaching at a slow pace, mounted on the very mare, for the possession of which he had for such a length of time sighed in vain. 'Esaaf,'—'help! good stranger,' he cried, with a faint voice, as though

the hand of the destroying angel had been upon
him.   'Do not desert a miserable being, who, but
for your kindly aid, must die the death of a dog.
Already I see the vultures hovering around to suck
the last drops of my freezing blood.   Help!—I
implore thee, by the love thou bearest thy own
life's blood!   Allah will reward thee, and thy days
shall end in peace!   By the beard of thy father,
do not desert thy fellow-man in his utmost need.
My eyes grow dim; for I have neither eaten nor
drunk for twenty-four hours.   Save me, or I die!'

"Now the chief Rejal el Hamed was a good
man, whose heart was always open to the distresses
of his fellow-creatures; so that the piteous tale of
the false-hearted Faris el Aanta wrought powerfully upon him.   'Thou shalt not perish,' he
exclaimed; 'get thee up behind me!   The pace of
my mare is greater than that of the whirlwind.
Get thee up behind me, and, with the speed of the
eagle, I will carry thee to my own tent, where thy
health shall be cared for, and where we will eat
together the salt of friendship.'

"'Alas!' cried the false chief, 'how shall I do
the thing thou askest of me?   My limbs are feeble;
my arms are as those of the nursling; and my legs

totter, as though my eyes had seen the sun of a
hundred summers. How, then, shall I do this
thing?'

" The kind-hearted sheikh, moved to compassion
at the well-feigned woe of his crafty rival, without
more ado, got down from his saddle, and proceeded to lift the supposed dying man, from the
ground; who, still keeping up the deception,
suffered himself to be raised, as though his strength
had actually deserted his limbs, and left him little
better than a lifeless mass. At last, by dint of
apparently great exertion, he was lifted into the
saddle; but, just as the good-hearted Rejal el
Hamed was about to mount likewise, to fulfil his
charitable promise, the ungrateful Faris el Aanta
siezed the bridle, struck his heel into the flank of
the fiery steed, and, before the astonished sheikh
could make any effort to stop him, galloped off
with his long wished for prize.

" When he had reached a short distance, he
heard the voice of the chief calling loudly upon
him to stop for one moment, so that he might
make a single request of him. Well knowing that
he now possessed the means of removing himself
out of his reach at a moment's warning, he reined

in the mare, and paused to hear what the request
of Rejal el Hamed might be.

" 'It is true, O false-hearted deceiver !' exclaimed
the sheikh—'It is true thou hast, by base artifices,
and by clothing thyself in the sacred garment
of poverty and distress, succeeded in robbing
me of that which I prized above all the riches
of the earth. The thing has come to pass; and who
shall quarrel with the will of destiny? " Takoun
aradet Allah"—" God's will be done !" But I
have one request to make of thee : which is, that
thou wilt speak of that which thou hast done to no
man. The mare thou hast got, and doubtless will
keep: but do not, I pray thee, tell to any one the
manner in which thou didst obtain possession of her.'

" The wiley chief, not understanding the reason
of this request, exclaimed 'Why asketh thou so
earnestly that I should tell no man concerning
this matter ?'

" ' Because,' replied the good sheikh, ' if thou
dost, there shall no longer be charity amongst
men : the hungry shall starve, and the sick shall
perish by the way-side, because no man will help
them ; for who will take unto his bosom the serpent
that seeketh his life's blood?'

"The artful Faris el Aanta was conscience-
stricken. He repented him of his foul purpose.
He descended from his saddle. He embraced the
good sheikh. He helped him to mount again his
much loved mare, and bade him farewell, saying
'Thou hast spoken the words of wisdom, O
sheikh: thou hast turned my soul from its foulness.
A moment since, and I was thine enemy. Behold,
I am become thy friend. Take thy mare. May
the blessings of Heaven attend thee; and may thy
years be as the sands of the desert!'"

To this a song succeeded, of a brisk and sprightly
character, in which the Turk of high degree was
held up to ridicule and contempt, on account of his
partiality for pale-faced Georgians. The first few
lines, as well as I recollect, ran as subjoined. The
melody is somewhat of the shortest.

The vocalist was succeeded by another narrator,
who, in his turn, gave place to a third; and thus
they proceeded, some telling of the desperate
encounters in which they or their friends had been
engaged, with the rival tribes; whilst others made
our hair stand on end with tales of fearful serpents,
of hideous aspect and enormous size. At length

BEDOUIN SONG.

(From the Arabic.)

A sleepy dog in the Bedouins tent, is the maid with the skin so fair;

The dark skin, brisk, in the Bedouin's tent, and like a jewel rare.

The Pasha loves his Georgian white, who costs him *kisses* many;

The Bedouin loves his dark eyed wife, who saves him many a penny.

The Georgian's eye sees but stone walls, and knows nor men nor nature.

The Bedouin's wife, wise as her lord, let none e'er think to cheat her.

The Georgian dull, the Bedouin gay the Pasha an old fool

Give us the wives that pitch our tents, and can a trig-ger pull.

Published by H. Colburn, Gt. Marlborough St.

the hour of eleven arrived, when the company
separated, each retiring to his couch, the members
of the sheikh's family and his guests to their
apartments in his tent, and the rest to their own
tents, in different parts of the encampment.

During the whole time these amusements lasted
not a word was uttered, not a sentiment expressed,
which could offend even the most fastidious;
while many of the tales were remarkable for
the high moral tone which pervaded them,
and which derived additional interest from the
simple and earnest manner in which they were
narrated.

With the rest, I also retired to the apartment
allotted to me; if I may venture to dignify the
little patch of ground, curtained off for my especial
use, by that name; but, for a long time, I was
totally unable to get a wink of sleep. The
novelty of my situation, so different from any
thing I had been accustomed to, with a carpet
instead of a comfortable matrass to lie upon, and
this, too, not spread on an elevated platform, but
laid upon the ground, combined with the constant
dread of venomous reptiles, which I expected to

feel every moment crawling over my body,
effectually expelled slumber from my eyelids,
notwithstanding the long ride I had had in the
early part of the day ; which, under other circumstances, would have made a sound night's rest a
matter of certainty.

I was not, however, doomed to suffer this
inconvenience long ; for no sooner did the kind-
hearted chief learn the condition in which I found
myself, according to the Bedouin fashion, than
he caused a bedstead of palm-tree wood to be
procured in an adjoining village not far from the
town of Hillah.

Having performed my devotions, I delivered
myself up to my reflections ; which, notwithstanding the scanty accommodations to which I
was obliged to conform myself, were far from
being of an unpleasing character. In the first
place, I had escaped from persecution. Here was
one cause of rejoicing. I had been received by
my hospitable host as a daughter ; and this alone,
after the continual jealousy and distrust to which I
had of late been exposed, would have made a bed
in the open desert, without rest or shelter, but sur-

rounded by kind friends, preferable to a couch of down in the walled city of calumny and persecution.

Here, if refreshing slumbers came not to renew my strength, no hideous dreams of past calamities haunted my troubled sleep, again holding up to my tortured senses, the mangled and bleeding forms of my murdered father and his ill-starred brothers. What are the horrors of the longest watch to visions such as these? The first impulse of thoughtfulness, upon waking, at finding that all these horrors were but a dream, was immediately checked by the terrible consciousness that the dread scenes through which a distempered imagination had, during the night, again carried me, had once, alas! a sad reality.

In a short time after my arrival at the encampment of the Dryaah tribe, instead of leaving my pillow with a throbbing heart, an aching head, and a disordered imagination, my tongue parched with thirst, and my eyes red and swollen with weeping, I rose early in the morning, with a cheerful heart and a serene mind, to enjoy the refreshing breezes of the early dawn.

Having devoted an hour to prayer, I walked
forth, and soon reached the banks of the majestic
Euphrates, along which I continued to stroll
until the sun rose above the horizon, unobscured
by a single cloud, tinging the vast encampment
with a most brilliant roseate hue, and darting its
rays, so as to make the bed of the rapid stream at
my feet as palpable as though no substance had
intervened between it and my vision; for the
water was clear as the purest crystal.

The air was filled with the bleating of sheep,
and the notes of thousands of living creatures,
sending forth, after their nature, hymns of praise
and thanksgiving to their Creator, and exulting in
the pride of existence. Anon, the encampment,
which had just before appeared dead as the
sepulchral mounds of departed greatness near
which it was pitched, swarmed with living beings,
busily engaged in preparing for the labours or
pleasures of the day. My heart was moved—my
soul was filled with gratitude—I involuntarily
broke forth in the language of the psalmist:—
" O Lord, how manifold are thy works; in wisdom
hast thou made them all; the earth is full of thy

riches!" After a delightful walk of two hours, I
returned to my private apartment in the tent of
the sheikh.

It was not long before I succeeded in winning
the good opinion of his wife, as well as that of his
mother, whose especial favourite I soon became.
Indeed, the impression made upon me by the
Bedouin women was of the most favourable kind.
They are, in general, well favoured, though
swarthy, with tall and well-developed figures,
remarkably slender waists, like the stem of the
palm-tree, without having recourse to artificial
means of compression, and small and delicately
formed hands and feet, showing as pure and as
thorough a breed as their fleet and highly prized
coursers. Their general height I should estimate
at about five feet six inches. Their hair is black
as the raven, and divided at the crown of the
head; part of it hanging down, in tresses innumerable, upon their shoulders behind, while the
other part is cut to the length of about two
inches, and combed straight over the forehead.

The prevailing nose ornament here is a large
gold ring hanging from the part separating the

nostrils, whereas the kharanfel or nose ornament
worn by the women of Assyria is fastened by
means of a hole pierced through the right nostril,
and consists of a round piece of gold with a small
jewel in the centre. This barbarous disfigurement
is the more to be regretted, as the ladies in question have, in most cases, been gifted by nature
with the true Grecian nose, following the perpendicular line of the forehead, and the deformity
cannot fail to shock the sense, which perhaps might
tolerate such decorations at the termination of the
low-bridged and turned up organ of the natives
farther east, where they may be supposed to be
employed for the purpose of checking the soaring
propensity of the upraised lip.

Their mouths are in general small, and their
teeth of a dazzling whiteness. They indulge,
nevertheless, in the hideous practice of staining
their skin with the juice of the indigo plant, which
they rub into punctures, made in various forms.
In the centre of the nether lip they make, by these
means, a perpendicular line of blue, round marks
on the centre of the chin and forehead, and an
ornament or flourish on each cheek. On the back

of both their hands, strange to say, they draw the
form of a cross, and upon each finger they make a
blue line, from the knuckle to the nail.

Their dress mostly consists of a chemise of blue
linen, descending from the shoulders to the feet.
In the case of the wives and female relatives of the
sheikhs, this part of the dress is frequently composed of red silk. Over the head is thrown a scarf,
the ends of which are twisted twice round the waist,
and a "mashallah," or cloak, of Persian wool embroidered with gold, in the case of a woman of
distinction, is thrown over the shoulders. Besides
these, they wear yellow boots, coming as high as
the knees, turned over at the top, somewhat after
the fashion of those worn by European cavalry
soldiers.

Their moral attributes are at least equal to their
physical perfections, and I must confess, much as
I have always found to admire in the character of
the male Bedouin, I am disposed to place that of
the female still higher; their courage, and power
of endurance, seemed to me in no way inferior to
that of their male companions; while their general
intelligence appeared much superior. Their warm
hearted kindness, and generous sympathy with

those of their own sex who may need their good
offices, without regard to difference of caste or
religious creed, I can bear witness to from close
observation and personal experience; and it has
inspired me with sentiments of gratitude towards
these untaught daughters of the desert, which no
length of time can efface.

The fact of my being a Christian never exposed
me either to injury or insult. I always sedulously
avoided any open parade of my religious observances, out of respect to the strong prejudice which
I well knew to be entertained by them against all
prescribed forms of worship whatever. They worship one God, who, they say, created all men
brothers, to render each other mutual assistance,
and to relieve the woes or distresses of one another.
They therefore look upon all subtle speculations
and nice points of doctrine with contempt, if not
with abhorrence; and they not unfrequently make
those who trouble their minds with such matters
feel the effects of their displeasure.

A mollah once paid a visit to the Dryaah tribe,
with the view, if possible, of turning the attention
of the unbelieving Arabs to the " kebleh," and
illumining the night of their souls with the moon-

shine of Islam. He neglected no advantage to be derived from outward show and circumstance, that could possibly tend to secure a successful issue to his pious mission. His venerable head was encircled by the green turban, the livery of the Prophet's own descendants, betokening the exalted mind which dwelt in the skull enveloped by it; while, to demonstrate how cheaply he held the pomp and splendour of this earthly sojourn, he rode into the encampment seated upon an ass.

The mollah concluded that nothing could withstand so well concerted a plan, seconded by so much pious humility. But the breast of the infidel is as the nether mill-stone! Green turban and ass were alike unavailing. He had no sooner commenced expounding, than he was assailed with shouts of derision and yells of displeasure. Nothing daunted, he proceeded to open the object of his coming amongst them, which was no other than a crusade, if I may so express it, against the Christians, whom, in good set language and with fiery denunciations, he pronounced unworthy to associate with the dogs of true believers. " Let us," he exclaimed, in an ecstacy of pious zeal, "drive out the unclean kafirs; let them no longer eat the salt

of your hospitality, nor stretch their unbelieving
limbs on the carpet of your misguided charity;
hunt them from your tents, if you would shield
your children from the curse of illegitimacy, and
your wives from pollution."

He had hardly concluded this stirring appeal,
when his congregation, roused to fury by this
last annunciation, seized the disconcerted mollah,
plucked him by the beard, in token of derision,
cut close this venerated appendage, and turned
him out of the camp, to be the laughing-stock of
wayfarers, and a warning to all mollahs ambitious
of propagating the true faith of the prophet among
the obdurate Arabs of the Euphrates.

Yet are these Arabs by no means destitute of
religious feelings. As I have already observed,
they believe in one God, the Creator of the universe, and the omnipotent disposer of human
events. To Him they attribute all their successes.
They never undertake any enterprize, without first
invoking his all-powerful aid. Their misfortunes
they likewise look upon as visitations of His divine
displeasure, and bear them without complaint or
murmur. Beyond this their piety does not extend.
As I have already stated, they view all religious

sects with equal abhorrence, and have themselves no regular practice of prayer.

The eyes of the Bedouin women are large, dark, and of great brilliancy; which is softened and subdued by long dark eyelashes, the effect of which they heighten by dying the eyelid, beneath the lash, with a powder consisting of indigo, mingled with some other substance; a mixture which is called in Arabic "kahal," applied by means of a "mil" or bodkin, which is attached to a bag called "jizdana," made of skin and filled with the kahal. This bodkin they first moisten, and then, having dipped it in the bag to which it is attached, they draw it under the eyelash, by which the softening effect of the long black lash is much increased. They profess to believe this practice calculated to preserve the eye from injury and disease; but I have no doubt that its strongest recommendation in the eyes of the Bedouin ladies, who doubtless are influenced by the wise instinct inherent in the minds of all the daughters of Eve, is its supposed power to enhance the force of their personal charms.

This practice must, I should imagine, be of very remote antiquity; for the sheikh gave me the

following enigma to unriddle, which, they maintain, was put by the Queen of Sheba to King
Solomon, when she went to hear the words of
wisdom from his inspired lips. "There was a well of
wood, which, instead of water, was filled with stones.
A drawer came ; who, having let down his bucket,
drew it up again, and carried the stones with
which it was filled to the water, that the water
might drink of them." I knit my brow, and for
some moments thought deeply what this might
signify; but being quite at a loss to divine the
enigma, I asked two hours time, which the sheikh
granted me. I ransacked my brain, and made
every effort to discover the meaning of the riddle,
but without success; the darkness still rested on
my soul, and I was forced to confess myself con-
quered. " But give me, O sheikh," I said, " till
to-morrow morning, and the knot of thy riddle shall
be untied." The sheikh laughed immoderately, and
granted me the delay I asked. I retired to my
apartment, and meditated long and deeply. Not
a wink of sleep did I get. At last the daylight
broke upon the darkness of my soul. I hastened
to the sheikh and said, " Thy hand-maiden hath
unfastened the knot, O sheikh ! The well of wood

is the 'jizdana,' the bucket is the 'mil,' the stones
with which it was filled are the berries from which
the kahal is made, and the water which shall drink
them is the liquid crystal which floats in the eye
of beauty."

" Ya sabhan Allah!"—" God be praised!" exclaimed the sheikh; "jenabki nabbia,"—" you are
a witch; who of our fathers could have done this
thing?"

The Bedouins entertain almost as strong an
aversion to books as they do to religious forms and
observances. I therefore always carefully avoided
making any display of the small collection I had
brought with me, never resorting to them except
when I was alone, and not likely to be disturbed.
I there frequently spent many an agreeable hour in
reading a book called "The Balance of Time:" a
work in which high moral principles are advocated
and aptly illustrated by powerfully drawn examples
of human virtue and human folly, and of the happiness to be derived from the one, and the inevit-
able misery consequent upon the other.

One day as I was engaged in the study of my
favourite book, I was surprised by the sudden
entrance of the sheikh's wife before I could contrive

to lay the volume, in the perusal of which I was so absorbed, aside. The curiosity of my hostess was excited. She desired to know what the book I was reading contained. Fearing that its contents were by no means likely to be pleasing to her, I replied, " Nothing—at least nothing in which you would feel any interest." She had, however, too much of the characteristic of her sex to be thus easily satisfied. The more mysterious I became, the more intense became her curiosity.

Unable any longer to resist her importunities, I turned over the leaves of my book, with the view of finding some passages likely to amuse and interest her. Avoiding any disquisitions on moral subjects, which I well knew could not be otherwise than distasteful to one accustomed to receive nearly all the information, moral and otherwise, which she acquired, through the medium of an anecdote or a tale, I lighted upon the following:

" A wanderer in the desert was once pursued by a hideous monster, having a single horn, strong and sharp, like the tusk of an elephant, projecting from the centre of his forehead. By dint of speed, which fear and terror had almost made supernatural, the fugitive had hitherto succeeded in

outstripping the dreaded beast, who was seeking
to devour him.   On he sped; every now and then
casting a terrified glance behind him, to see if his
hideous adversary was still following in his track.
He saw the object of his dread at the same distance
from him as before.   All his efforts to gain upon
him had been fruitless.   The samiri of the desert
opposed its fiery breath in vain.   The hunted
traveller heeded it not; for death stared him in
the face.

" His strength now began to fail him.   It was
clear that he could but for a little time longer
escape the dire fate which hung over his devoted
head; for the monster was gaining fast upon him.
His jaws were already opened wide to tear his
victim to pieces; his eyes glared like two furnaces
with fierce exultation; when the traveller came
suddenly upon a ditch, into which he dropped,
more dead than alive.

" Now on one side of this ditch grew a stately
tree.   The infuriated beast no sooner saw the
wretched fugitive couching in this ditch, than,
with a loud and dreadful roar, he plunged in after
him.   But the traveller had espied this tree, and
when he saw the monster taking the leap, with

the strength of desperation, he scrambled up in
it until he was fairly out of the reach of his
assailant.

" His heart was filled with rejoicing and gratitude to God for his miraculous deliverance; for
he felt as one who had been plucked from the
jaws of death.   Having, in some degree, recovered
from his terror, he had now leisure to look around
him.   The rejoicing which had so rapidly succeeded his past fears, was, alas! soon followed by
fears of another description.   True, he had escaped
the devouring jaw of the fell monster who sought
to destroy him; but how was he to support that
life which had been preserved by means so wonderful? for whenever he cast his eyes about him,
he beheld his enemy glaring upon him from the
ditch below.

" Looking still further around him, he perceived
two odious huge rats, one white, the other black,
who were busily engaged in growing the roots of
the tree upon the branches of which he had found
an asylum; while on the other side he encountered
the hateful gaze of four enormous serpents, which
lay coiled up, eagerly waiting for the fall of the
tree.   Beyond these was a terrible dragon of the

size of an elephant, which also seemed waiting to devour him.

" 'Alas! alas!' cried the unhappy man, wringing his hands in agony, 'what will become of me? Woe is me, for my destiny is evil. But a little while since, I thought myself saved from one frightful calamity, and now I see myself encompassed with danger on every side. What, then, does it matter, whether I become the prey of the gaping monsters around me, or perish of hunger before their eyes? There is no escape for me! Woe is me, that ever I was born!'

" At length, when he had exhausted himself with lamentation, on a sudden his tears were turned to joy, as he espied a bee-hive on a branch above him, and quickly making towards it, restored his sinking energies with its delicious contents· Again his spirit was changed. He turned his eyes no more below him. He no more heeded the dangers which environed him on every side. He thought only of enjoying the sweets which his lucky stars had so providentially placed within his reach; and he thus passed away his time, heedless of the future, until the tree upon which he rested, gnawed through by the unceasing efforts of the

two rats, at length fell, without a moment's warning, and delivered the traveller into the jaws of
his fell destroyer."

In this parable is figured the life of man. The
desert spoken of is this world. The unicorn
is death, which ever walks by the side of man,
from his cradle to his last hour. Whether waking
or sleeping, in motion, or at rest, from sunrise to
sunset, and from its going down to its uprising.
The four serpents are the four elements, the
instruments of disease and destruction, robbing
man of health, and sweeping away, in their headlong and resistless course, alike the old and the
young. The white rat is day, the black rat
night; which silently but incessantly gnaw our
lives from under our feet, until the sapless trunk
at length falls, and delivers up its tenant to the
jaws of the dragon, which is eternity. The
honey is the pleasures and seductions of this
world; and woe, eternal woe to him who, like
the careless traveller who had so lately escaped
from the jaws of death, recklessly devotes himself
to its enjoyments, heedless of the dangers which
encompass him on every side.

"It is very good," exclaimed the sheikh's wife,

when I had concluded, "these things are true, and pleasant to the ear." Then, thanking me with great warmth and cordiality, for the entertainment I had afforded her, she took her leave.

Not long after this she returned, bringing with her several of her female friends and acquaintances, and said to me, " Tell, O Amira these women, the things thou toldest me out of the book, which is as an emerald mine for its store of riches, and their hearts shall be filled with joy." I agreed to go through the story again, upon one condition, which was, that we should make a party to hunt gazelles. In making this stipulation I had two objects in view; one was the enjoyment of the sport, of which I was excessively fond, and the other, my unconquerable dislike of the flesh of the camel, which always formed a prominent part of our fare. I therefore promised to go through the whole story, when we should repose after our day's sport in the Desert. Upon the following day we indulged in our favourite pastime ; and accordingly, in the evening, I redeemed my pledge, by again reading the parable which had so greatly pleased the sheikh's wife.

On returning from our daily excursions I often amused myself for hours in playing with the young camels; which are as playful as their elders are grave. One of these, only fifteen days old, was an especial favourite of mine. It was excessively frolicksome, and knew me as well as it did its own mother. It would take its food from my hand, and show other marks of its confidence and attachment to me. On seeing me approach it would leap like a kitten, and run to hide itself in sport.

The camel is regarded as a sacred animal by the Arabs, and treated with great consideration; for, with great truth, they say, " Without our camels we should not have food nor drink, neither should we have wherewithal to clothe ourselves." The flesh of the camel furnishes them with food, when no other can be had; its milk, besides supplying them with cheese, affords, as it were, an inexhaustible fountain, where, without it, the Arab must perish of thirst on the parched desert. The camels set apart for the purposes of food are white, and are neither loaded nor subjected to labour of any kind.

After a few days stay with the Dryaah tribe,

I became acquainted with the principal members of all the neighbouring tribes, by whom I was, on every occasion on which I visited them, treated with the greatest kindness, hospitality, and distinction; and at this distance of time, gratitude compels me to declare my conviction, that more real friends are to be made in one day amongst these lawless tribes, than could be formed in a century in civilized Europe, where it is possible to live for half a century without knowing your neighbour.

Whatever may be the defects in the Bedouin character, assuredly luke-warm friendship is not one. An attachment once formed, continues through life. In every change of fortune, they cheerfully share their last crust with those to whom they have sworn eternal friendship. Even their bitterest enemy, if overwhelmed with misfortune, is not excluded from their wide-spread hospitality. Violations of it are punished with death. An instance of this, which occurred in the Dryaah tribe, was related to me. A stranger, who had been a guest of this tribe, after quitting their encampment, placed himself under the protection of a neighbouring tribe; by some

members of which he was himself maltreated,
and his slave killed. The Dryaah tribe, on
becoming acquainted with this outrage, this gross
violation of the Bedouin laws, immediately made
war on their neighbours, and avenged the injury
done to their guest. The person of their greatest
enemy is ever held sacred, should he seek their
tents and claim their protection.

It is impossible to live for any length of time
amongst this people, without becoming sensible of
the height to which the rare virtues of friendship
and hospitality, not the mere parade of them,
having for its object rather the gratification of the
pride of the giver than the solace of the receiver,
are carried.

While I resided with the Dryaah tribe, I was
told of an instance of hospitality, which appears to
me scarcely inferior to that recorded in holy writ,
where the prophet was relieved by the kind
charity of the pious widow. The principal actor
in this case was also a widow, whose children had
all been cut off in a fray with a neighbouring
tribe; so that she was left, in her old age, without
stay or prop, and with barely a sufficiency for her
subsistence.

It chanced one day, that two travellers, worn with fatigue, and fainting from thirst and hunger, passed the door of her tent. They were Indians, and on their way to Damascus. The widow, who was sitting before her tent, seeing the pitiable condition of the famished travellers, invited them to repose within, and refresh themselves with what fare she had to offer, saying " See, I have yet a sheep left, which we will straightway kill, that your hunger may be stayed: bread I have none, but there are those around who will give it me; tarry here, therefore, while I hasten to fetch it.

The travellers, seeing that the widow was poor, and had but this one sheep, would have gone away, preferring to suffer yet awhile the pangs of hunger, rather than diminish her scanty store. But the widow heeded them not. She killed her sheep; she sought bread amongst her neighbours: and setting the provisions before them, she said : " Wherefore would ye have grieved me by going away empty? for if ye meet not with hospitality in the tents of the living, it had been as well if ye had sought succour in the graves of the dead. Shall not the Almighty render me that which I

give an hundred fold? Allah kerim!"—" God is
merciful!"

Seeing daily so many admirable virtues mani-
fested in the conduct of my Bedouin hosts, I was
much tempted to make some efforts towards their
conversion to the true faith, and to induce them
to study Catholic books. I even went so far as to
baptise a few children in secret; but I was unsuccessful. Their settled dislike to all established
forms of worship, and their aversion to books in
general, completely baffled all my efforts. I went
to as great lengths as I dared. I spoke to them of
a future state; of the rewards which would attend
the virtuous hereafter; and of the punishments
which would await the wicked. Often had I the
commandment "Thou shalt not steal," at the tip
of my tongue, but fear prevented my giving it
utterance. Many of the other divine commandments I found they knew, and what was still
better, constantly practised.

CHAPTER VIII.

An Arab Encampment in motion—An Arab Feast—The late
Duke of Orleans—Anecdote—A Marriage in the Desert—
Singular Ceremonies—A Wedding Procession and Feast—
Worship in the Desert—The Legend of St. Anthony.

I HAD not been many weeks in the camp, when
the whole tribe were in commotion. I beheld
men and women rushing to and fro—shepherds
collecting their flocks—camels in constant motion
backwards and forwards throughout the encampment; the saddling of horses, and the striking of
tents, all showed that we were about to shift our
quarters, and go in quest of fresher pastures.
While the men were engaged in getting ready
their fiery steeds, which filled the air with their
neighings, the women were busy in striking the
tents, and packing them and the domestic furni-

ture on the backs of the camels destined for this
service.

Never did I witness so bustling a scene. Every
thing was in motion—every soul was busily occupied. Never in my life had I beheld so many
beautiful horses at one time. As far as the eye
could reach in one direction, they were to be seen
prancing, pawing the ground, and neighing in
their joy, as though they were conscious that they
were about to exchange their exhausted fields
for new pastures. The very camels of burden,
poor beasts! with mountains of baggage on their
backs, seemed to rejoice; while their young ones
capered around them, apparently wondering at the
apathy of their more sober dams.

When the tents had been safely packed, the
flocks collected, and all was ready for departure,
we set out in the following order:—In the front
rode the men, mounted on their high-mettled
coursers; a formidable band, completely armed,
with their long lances gracefully poised, the points
of which, raised high in air, glittered and sparkled
in the sun.

Next in order came the women; the most considerable of whom rode each in a "maharah," a

canopy with curtains around it, placed on the
back of a dromedary, attended by their slaves and
negresses, who were also mounted on camels. I
had selected for my own use the tallest camel,
that I might the better enjoy the prospect.

After the women and their attendants came the
baggage-camels, bearing the tents, provisions, and
effects of the tribe; and countless flocks, tended
by their shepherds, brought up the rear.

In this order we proceeded, halting every two
hours to take coffee; and, as we rode along, men
accompanied us on foot, loaded with roasted meats,
bread, and dates, crying aloud, " He who is hungry,
let him approach."

Towards evening, we reached the place of our
destination, on the banks of the Nahr el Kashoun,
a spot abounding in fat pastures, and not far from
the Euphrates.   Here again was a scene of bustle,
similar to that I had witnessed in the morning.
Every one applied himself to his duty with alacrity
and assiduity; for all were anxious for the grand
feast, which our sheikh had announced his intention to give on our arriving at our new quarters.

This entertainment was upon a scale worthy of
the station of our hospitable entertainer. Seven

camels, twenty-five sheep, besides gazelles without number, were slaughtered upon the occasion. After the tents had been pitched, the flocks tended, and the horses stalled and fed with camel's milk, which is supposed by the Bedouins to give them great strength and power of endurance, our table was spread on the grass, close by the river's bank, and the dinner placed before us. Some of the dishes would have made an European open his eyes with wonder; being so large as to require four men to carry them, filled with rice, which looked like mountains, on which were placed lambs or sheep, roasted whole. All these dishes were of a white, shining substance, having the appearance of silver, but I did not learn of what metal they were made. There were also huge dishes, each containing a joint of camel's flesh, and others filled with gazelles, my favourite dish. We had, moreover, a dish called sambusak; which is a mixture of burnt flour, with honey, and butter, enveloped in a crust made square, which is rolled out very thin. The mixture is put in the centre, the four corners are turned over crossways, and the dish is then baked.

I have seldom enjoyed a meal more than I did

the dinner given by our sheikh upon this occasion, on the banks of the Euphrates. I thought every thing good, except the camel joints, the red flesh and coarse flavour of which I never could endure : and it appeared to me at that moment, that under no circumstances which could by possibility befall me, should I be able to contemplate the idea of making a meal of it without horror. But I was mistaken. Many years after, when my lot cast me, not in the company of Bedouin Arabs, but amidst European Christians, in one of the strong-holds of civilization, surrounded by wealth and plenty on every side, I was cured of my fasti-diousness. As the facts referred to made a very deep impression on my mind, I hope I shall be excused for stating them in this place, as the moral they convey is an instructive one.

At the period I am alluding to, I resided in one of the largest capitals of Europe. I had hired a very humble apartment, in an establishment be-longing to a noble lady, whose fortune had been acquired in the East. Through a succession of misfortunes, I had lost all I possessed. I was, indeed, reduced to the bitterest penury; my only means of subsistence being derived from a pupil,

to whom I had been recommended by the late
lamented and truly kind hearted Duke of Orleans,
whose untimely fate has robbed many an unfortunate of his only true friend, to whom I was in
the habit of giving two lessons a week in Arabic,
and for which he paid me at the rate of three
francs a lesson.   For some time I had been endeavouring to procure a subsistence by this means;
for I could teach several Oriental languages; but
this was my only pupil.   Small, however, as this
pittance was, I determined to make an endeavour to live upon it, rather than submit to the
humiliation of seeking assistance at the hands of
my acquaintances.

As my means narrowed, I gradually lessened
my allowance of food, until, at length, it was so
reduced in quantity as to be scarcely sufficient to
keep body and soul together.   For months I had
allowed myself only one meal a day.   It consisted
of a little semolina boiled in water, by the aid of a
spirit-lamp (for I had no means of purchasing
fuel), and a small portion of bread.

My case now became desperate; for I had a
sum equal to twenty shillings a month to pay for
my lodging, and my income did not exceed five

shillings a week, the fee of two lessons, which I gave every Tuesday and Friday. Thus week after week passed over my head. Every day the cold hand of poverty tightened his grasp. The fountains of my blood were almost frozen to ice: I was as a shadow. My voice had nearly forsaken me; I was with difficulty able to walk.

One day—never shall I forget it! it was one of those upon which I was in the habit of going to my pupil, who lived in a fashionable part of the town—I had eaten nothing for thirty hours; for I had nothing remaining wherewith to purchase a morsel of bread. I waited with all the impatience of pinching hunger for the hour at which my pupil was in the habit of taking his lesson. It was in the depth of as bitter a winter as ever visited that city. The snow was lying thick upon the ground, and the river was frozen hard, on the day, when, scarcely able to crawl, I set out in the full confidence of receiving the price of my labour, with which I purposed to buy food to save myself from starvation.

At length I arrived at the residence of my pupil. But what were my sensations, on being told by him, that he had accepted an invitation to a ball, and consequently could not take a lesson that evening. He made a thousand apologies for the trouble he had given me, and was, I have no doubt, sincere in his protestations. But what frightful words were these to one whose life hung upon the miserable pittance which she expected to receive. My heart sank within me. His voice sounded like my death knell. I know not what I said; but I left him, and again found myself treading the deep snow, while every blast seemed to freeze my blood and to chill my very bones.

In this dreadful extremity my pride gave way. I determined to endeavour to borrow a small trifle from some of my friends. The first to whom I applied dismissed me with a civil excuse; and the others, as I was told, were not at home. Thus baffled and heart-broken I returned homewards, for I had now no refuge save in God, to whom I committed myself. I lifted up my eyes to heaven and cried, " Thou, O Lord! art my hope and refuge in my distress." I reached my lodgings, and I tottered up to my cheerless apartment. I was several times forced to stand aside to make room for the servants of the opulent individual, in whose hotel I lodged, and who were constantly passing between the kitchen and their master's apartment; for there was a great feast and merry-making. Reader! picture to yourself my feelings at that moment. On reaching my room I threw myself on my bed. I prayed for death; for the pangs of hunger and humiliation now racked my body and soul. I bethought me of the hospitable meals I had seen spread at my father's table. O how correct was Dante, the great interpreter of nature and of human feelings, when he put these sorrowful words into the mouth of the ill-fated and suffering Francesca di Rimini:—" Nessun maggior dolore che ricordarsi del tempo felice nella miseria."

I longed for the broken remains which I had so often seen given away to the poor and destitute. Oh, how I sighed at that moment of dire necessity for a morsel of that camel's flesh, which, while I resided in the tent of those hospitable Bedouins, I had looked upon with so much loathing! With what eagerness could I have devoured the coarse, red flesh I have been speaking of in that sad hour! After passing the long winter night in excruciating torments, I availed myself of the first ray of light to address a letter to a lady to whom I had been able to render some service, and who had always concluded her letters to me with the glowing words, " Your sincere friend till death." In order to make sure that my letter would reach its destination, I gave it to a commissionaire to carry, promising him payment on his return, for I relied with confidence on my warm-hearted friend. To guard against the possibility of disappointment, I also gave him a second letter to another friend, requesting a temporary loan.

No answer, however, being returned to either, I was compelled to sell a relic which I always carried about with me, a present from his holiness the Pope, and which I highly prized; for it was reputed to be a piece of the true cross, enclosed in a box of pure gold, the only article of value I had remaining, in order to pay the commissionaire and procure myself a meal.

But, to return to my narration. Not long after our settlement at Nahr el Kashoun, our sheikh received an invitation from a neighbouring tribe to attend a marriage which was about to take place amongst them. The parties betrothed being persons of high birth, vast preparations had been

made for the due celebration of so important an
event, and invitations had been sent to all the
surrounding chieftains, with their relations and
friends to be present.

The mode of contracting marriages amongst the
Bedouin tribes is singular and amusing. The
enamoured swain, accompanied by his parents
and friends, pays a visit to the tent of his beloved's
father. Habitually the Bedouins, it is well known,
are models of politeness; courtesy and friendly
offices being enjoined among them by strict laws,
the violation of which is punished with the greatest
severity. When, however, the visit is understood
to be paid for the purpose of making a proposal
of marriage, they studiously avoid showing the
slightest mark of respect or common courtesy to
their visitors; and will not even rise from their
seats upon their entrance. Under such delicate
circumstances, they consider any appearance of
eagerness as highly derogatory, and adopt this
seemingly rude behaviour, by way of showing
their independence.

One of the would-be bridegroom's friends then
opens the negotiation, in somewhat after the following manner:—" Wherefore," he exclaims, " do

you receive us thus coldly? We have neither taken your Nedjd mares, nor have we shed the blood of your young men. If ye have forgotten the duties of hospitality, we will straightway return to our tents."

During this address, the young lady, whose hand is the object of the visit, is occupied in scrutinizing through a hole in the curtain, which separates the female from the male apartment, the features and person of the candidate for her affections. Should the youth not possess sufficient attractions for the lady, she makes a preconcerted sign, by which the parents know that he is not the object of her choice; and thereupon the party are suffered to depart, without any act of civility being shown them, or apology made.

If, however, the case should be otherwise; if the signal should be that the youth has been seen and approved of, then the demeanour of the lady's friends undergoes an immediate change; forbidding looks are replaced by smiles; cold incivility is succeeded by the warmest professions of friendship. —" Ahalan w' sahalan,"—" you are welcome,' exclaims the father: " Halat elbarakah fikum,"— " a benediction descends upon us when you are

present,"—" Not only will we show you hospitality, but ye shall have all ye desire; ask and ye
shall be gratified; our wealth is yours, and we are
your slaves."

To this the friends of the youth reply,—" We
are come to ask of thee the hand of thy daughter
for our friend, whom thou seest by our side; tell us,
therefore, O sheikh, the portion which thou askest
for her." They then proceed to business in earnest,
and, without the aid of lawyers, settle the portion
of the bride; how many " nakas," a sort of camel
for riding; how many blood horses; how many
sheep, negroes and negresses; how many pairs of
yellow boots; and, lastly, the amount of presents
to be made to the bride's friends and relations.
All these weighty matters are speedily arranged,
when once the lady has signified her approval.

I have said that the parties to whose espousals
we were invited were persons of distinction. The
lady had but a little while before received the distinguished honour of being appointed hafta of her
tribe, in a war in which they had been engaged
with a neighbouring horde. When a tribe is about
to engage in war with another, they seek out the
most beautiful virgin they can find amongst their

people, or amongst friendly tribes, to be their hafta.
She must also excel all others in courage and elo-
quence, for her post is in the front rank, and her
duty is to excite her followers, by her glowing
appeals, to feats of valour.

The hafta is regarded by her surrounding warriors with a sort of religious reverence, as holding,
in a manner, the issues of fate in her hand; and
goes forth to battle seated on the largest and most
beautifully white female camel that can be found.
Her " maharah," is covered with scarlet cloth, and
decorated with all sorts of ornamental devices, with
a deep fringe of gold. She is always seen in the
thickest of the fight, and surrounded by the most
renowned warriors of her tribe, whom she animates
and encourages by her voice and gestures; calling
on the old and tried ones to remember their former
glorious deeds, and stimulating the young to pro-
digies of valour, by promising her hand to the
fortunate youth who shall bring the head of the
enemy's general.

Half the force is set apart for the protection of
the hafta, and all the ambitious spirits of the tribe
are found at her side ; for despair seizes the warriors,
and the battle is inevitably lost, should she fall into

the hands of the enemy. Before the conflict com-
mences, each warrior presents himself in turn to
the hafta, and asks her to inspire him with courage
and enthusiasm, saying, " O most beautiful among
the beautiful! for thee I go to battle; my life is
thine; let me behold the brightness of thy face,
that the heart of thy slave may be filled with courage, so that his voice may be as the lion's roar in
the ears of the enemy, and his lance as the destroying angel." To which the hafta replies, " Go,
brave youth! be thy heart as that of the lion, and
thy lance as the wide spread pestilence. I am the
hafta, the reward of the bravest of the brave; and
my price is the head of the enemy's chief."

In a war which had taken place a short time
before, I was told the hafta was the daughter of a
chief, whose tents were at no great distance from
our encampment. A relation of a neighbouring
sheikh had laid the head of the opposing chief at
her feet, and had claimed his privilege. Arrangements were immediately made for the celebration
of the marriage between the young hero and the
sheikh's daughter, in a manner worthy of their
blood and high achievements; and it was to this
wedding that we were invited.

The Bedouins, who are in general extremely simple in their attire, upon marriage ceremonies depart from their usual custom, and appear in dresses of considerable magnificence, composed, I am inclined to suspect, entirely of the spoils taken from merchants who had never the remotest intention that they should be so employed. A little difficulty enterposed, in my case. I had no dresses but such as I had been in the habit of wearing at Bagdad; which were not, by any means, fitted for such festive occasions. However, as I was most anxious to be present at a Bedouin marriage, both from curiosity to observe their customs upon so interesting an occasion, and a wish to seek distraction from melancholy reflections, I had a dress made up for the occasion, and went to the feast attired as a Bedouin woman.

The finest mares in the sheikh's stud were saddled for our use, and we started at day-break for the encampment of the bridegroom's father, who was related to our sheikh, which was about three hours distance from the Dryaah camp, in a party consisting of about twenty persons, including slaves.

We soon reached the tents of our host, who
had taken up his position on a spot abounding in
rich pastures, over which were spread flocks, horses,
and camels, in numbers bespeaking the wealth of
the owner; whilst the countless peaks of the tents
stretching far and wide over the plain, presented
the appearance of a city of camels hair. I am
sure I counted, as we approached the encampment, not fewer than a thousand tents.

We rode straight to the centre of them, where
the tent of Faris el Hamadan, the bridegroom's
father, was pitched, and were received at the
door by a great number of females, who came out
to meet us, and greeted us with the utmost cordiality and respect. Our hostess conducted us
into the sheikh's tent, saying, at the same time,
"Anastuna sharaftuna," the customary compliment on receiving a visitor to whom honour is
due, which means, "you have civilized us; you
have done us honour," and ordered coffee to be
brought. Here, again, the kindness of my friends
procured for me a dispensation from the rigid
observance of the Bedouin law, which prohibits
indulgence in the use of the "accursed weed,"
as they call tobacco; and I was, through the

intervention of the Sheikh Dryaah Ebn Shalan's daughter, permitted to enjoy my favourite nerghila.

After dinner we made a cheerful and merry evening of it; passing our time in dancing, singing, and relating stories till midnight. The next morning we rose at daybreak, and prepared to visit the encampment of the bride's father, which was at a very short distance. Long before sunrise all was ready, and shortly after we set out in the following order:—

Foremost of all rode a single cavalier, mounted on a splendidly caparisoned mare, bearing in his hand a byrakh, or flag, the pole of which must have been not less than fifteen or sixteen feet in length, I should say; for, when resting on the ground, the head of the horseman barely reached its middle. On the top of it floated a white flag, and as the procession proceeded on its way, the standard bearer every now and then cried aloud, " We go to seek honour without stain."

Next were ranged the camels, forming part of the bride's portion, covered with garlands and branches gathered on the banks of the Euphrates, with their drivers. These were followed by a

negro slave, also part of the dower, superbly
dressed, and mounted on horseback, surrounded
by men on foot, who marched forward carolling
songs of joy and gladness. Then came a troop of
mounted warriors, completely armed, curvetting
on their high-couraged blood-horses, and dis-
charging, from time to time, their muskets in
the air. After the warriors, followed a band of
females, bearing censers filled with sweet incense,
scattering fragrance through the air; who were
succeeded by large flocks of sheep, part of the
bride's portion, tended by their shepherds, who,
as they trudged along merrily by the side of their
charge, lustily chanted a song, beginning with the
words, " Thus did Chibouk, the brother of Antar,
two thousand years ago," by way of asserting the
attachment of the Bedouins to the usages of their
ancestors.

Then followed the negresses, destined to be the
slaves of the bride, richly dressed, surrounded by
about two hundred men on foot, dancing and
singing all kinds of songs, as they marched in front
of the camel bearing the bride's *trousseau.* This
was an uncommonly large beast, and seemed to
have been selected for the purpose of having as

much surface as possible for the display of the
wedding presents; which were hung all over the
camel, presenting an appearance not unlike that
of a pedlar's cart, with the wares exposed in
a manner most likely to fascinate and attract
purchasers.

All sorts of valuable ornaments were arranged
in sparkling festoons. Mashallahs, covered with
gold embroidery, were spread over the well-filled
skin of the animal; while a graceful filagree work
was produced by the skilful arrangement of the
many pairs of yellow jack boots, which hung suspended in every direction. After the *trousseau,*
followed a child about eight years old, a scion of
one of the most distinguished Bedouin families,
mounted on a camel, who cried, in a loud voice,
" May our people ever be victorious!—may the
fire of our enemies never be quenched!" To
which another child, who accompanied him, cried
" Amen!" And in this manner, amidst shouting,
singing, and rejoicing, we at length reached the
tent of the hafta's father.

Here we were met with corresponding songs
and rejoicings by the bride's friends. The camel
bearing the *trousseau* was unladen, and the costly

load deposited in the tent around the "rabha," or reception-room. which, upon this occasion, was adorned with a splendid Persian carpet spread on the ground. Coffee was then served up from a mighty cauldron; for the preparations were all upon a gigantic scale; and when we had refreshed ourselves with this and with camel's milk, which was also brought in, the company proceeded to pray, after their fashion, for the future welfare of the wedded pair.

We shortly after sallied forth into the desert, in two parties; the friends of the bride forming one, and those of the bridegroom the other. Having reached the appointed place, the young men on each side separated themselves from their friends, and arranged themselves in two bodies in battle array, while the elders took up a position from which they could behold the manœuvres.

A mock engagement now ensued, for the possession of the hafta; which was suffered to terminate in favour of the bridegroom's party, who carried her off in triumph, and confided her to the care of the bridegroom's female relatives and their friends. She was then surrounded by a great number of young virgins, who accompanied her to the door of her tent, where her camel was waiting ready saddled, and more richly caparisoned than ever. Over his glossy back, which was as white as snow, was thrown a huge saddle-cloth of scarlet, having a deep fringe of many-coloured worsted. The head of the animal was decorated with ostrich feathers, and her bandeau sparkled with many-coloured glass and embroidery; while small mirrors, hung here and there on different parts of her body, reflected the splendour of the passing scene, and sent forth flashes of light as they caught the rays of the sun.

The maharah, or pavilion, on the camel's back, was spread with a rich Persian carpet, on which were thrown cushions covered with silk. Into this the bride was assisted by the bridegroom's female friends, who then arranged themselves in order, some mounted on camels, and some on foot, singing as they went, to accompany her to the tent of her husband.

While these preparations were going on, a party of the bridegroom's friends galloped forward to announce the speedy arrival of the bride at the tent of the bridegroom's tribe. The bridal procession now moved onward towards its final destination, amidst songs of triumph and exultation. Some well-wishers, more enthusiastic than the rest, sacrificed sheep at the feet of the camel on which the bride was seated, as a votive offering of propitiation.

After the camel on which the bride's maharah was placed, followed two others; one of which carried her tent and furniture, and the other the Persian carpet and kitchen utensils. In this order they arrived at the bridegroom's tent, into which the bride was conducted; and the whole ceremony concluded with a dinner, upon a scale of magnitude such as I never before witnessed.

Next morning, the interchange of presents took place; the husband, with very few exceptions, being at the whole expense. That I might not disgrace my liberal friends, I presented the bride with a "jisdana" and golden "mil," the apparatus used for heightening the effect of the eyelash, as already described, together with a necklace and bracelets of amber.

To me the bride presented an emerald of considerable value and of large size, set in a ring, and an ample Persian shawl, descending from the shoulders to the feet, made entirely of the finest

Cashmere wool; which, notwithstanding its size, could be held in the palm of the hand, and which I afterwards sold at Rome for two hundred scudi, when under the pressure of dire necessity. Added to these, was a valuable necklace, consisting of three rows of the finest pearls. Singularly enough, the Bedouins have not the most remote idea of the value of such articles, and will frequently exchange diamonds worth thousands of francs, for a sack of dates worth not more than five, and Persian shawls of great beauty and value for a bag of rice.

Thoroughly appreciating, as I did, the kind motive which prompted the hafta in making me this sumptuous present, and fearful as I naturally was of doing anything calculated to give offence to those at whose hands I had received so much kind attention, I could still hardly reconcile myself to accept the proffered treasures; for I had something rather stronger than a shrewd suspicion, that they had been acquired in the plunder of a caravan, which had been attacked by this tribe, on its annual journey from Bassorah to Damascus, by way of Bagdad, not long before.

While I was turning these considerations over

in my mind, it occurred to me, that an uncle of mine had lost some valuable jewels, which had been sent by this very caravan; and thus, firmly resolving to restore the precious gifts to their rightful owners, if Providence should ever throw them in my way, I managed to still the scruples of conscience—a rather temporizing species of morality, I must confess.

We remained three days with this tribe; during the whole of which time little was thought of but eating and drinking, dancing and singing. A large fire was lighted, before which they arranged themselves in a vast circle, consisting of not fewer than fifty persons, and continued dancing round and round, each holding his neighbour by the hand; the musicians, with their tambours and pipes, being stationed in the centre.

Never did I see a more happy assemblage. Everybody seemed bent on enjoying himself, without thought of the morrow. Some of the stories told, and the antics played, by the Bedouins, were enough to make the gravest individual die with laughter. As for me, I had no spirit for such diversions. Often, out of mortification at finding my own the only sad countenance in the midst of

so many joyous faces, I rushed from the merry
strains of the happy crowd to seek refuge in
solitude.

The festivities being over, we bade adieu to our
friends, and having wished every happiness to the
wedded pair, we set out on our return to our own
encampment. When we had settled ourselves, I
resumed my former mode of life, rising early, and
going every morning into the desert alone, and
performing my devotions in its peaceful solitude,
unseen by all but that great Being, to whom, in
deep humility, I offered up praise and adoration.

One morning I wandered on the bank of a
canal which flowed into the Euphrates, deeply
engaged in reading my favourite book, my soul
filled with enthusiasm by its powerful appeals to
the better part of our nature, and unconscious of
all earthly objects. For some time past, I had
discontinued the practice to which, from infancy,
I had been accustomed, of praying upon my knees,
out of consideration for the prejudices of my hosts.
The chapter I was reading painted in such glowing colours the beauty of the Almighty towards
man, and gave so fearful, but at the same time,
so just a picture of man's ingratitude for all the

benefits conferred upon him, that I was moved to
tears, and falling upon my knees, with my eyes
upraised to heaven, I implored the assistance of
the Holy Ghost to give me strength to feel fully
and to acknowledge the goodness of God towards
me.

I was young and enthusiastic, with a warm
imagination and unsuspecting temperament; but
it seemed to me, as I raised my eyes to heaven,
that a light shot forth, which so dazzled me, that I
remained transfixed to the spot. As I thus knelt,
unconscious of all surrounding objects, I was
aroused from my trance by the voices of my
Bedouin female friends, who, from a distance,
seeing me fall upon my knees, being apprehensive
that some evil had befallen me, had hastened to
my succour, and now, with anxiety and alarm
depicted in their countenances, inquired of me
what was the matter.

" It is nothing," I replied ; " I am now well."

" How is it, then," asked one of them, " my
friend, that we saw thee but now fall down, as
though the samiri had entered thy nostrils? These
things are strange : we cannot understand them."

What was now to be done? I was discovered

I scorned to tell a falsehood upon any occasion;
and to dissemble, under such circumstances, would
be, I felt, the height of impiety. I could not,
indeed, reflect upon the dissimulation of which I
had already been guilty, without a pang of remorse; for my conscience told me that it almost
amounted to a denial of my Creator, as though I
had been ashamed of His worship.

" Oh that it were given me," I inwardly prayed,
"to be the humble instrument for the conversion of
these simple-minded children of nature to the true
worship of thee, my God! so that these things
which, even now, they do from the impulses which
thy almighty goodness has implanted in their hearts,
they might perform for the glory and honour of thy
holy name! Are not thy commandments written
in the hearts of all men, although sometimes well
nigh blotted out by the foul stains of barbarism
and degrading superstition? I will confess my
heavenly Father to these children of error. Peradventure I may be the means of turning their
hearts to a just knowledge of His mercy, and teach
their tongues to sing the glory of His holy name."

" My friends," I said to them, " sickness has
not deprived my knees of their wonted strength,

neither has the withering samiri dried up the
fountains of my blood. The cause of that which
you have seen lies in that little book."

" What words are these?" cried the women.
" Who ever saw one struck down to the earth by
such a thing? We understand thee not; unless it
be that thy book contains a talisman."

" It is a talisman; it is a talisman," exclaimed
many voices at once. " Let us see; let us see!"

" Indeed there is no talisman here," I said; " in
this book there is no power, save that possessed
by the word of truth. There is no talisman here.
Ye shall judge for yourselves; for I will read to
you the words of the book." Immediately they
all flocked around me, with eager curiosity painted
on their faces, as, opening it at random, I proceeded
to read to them the following legend:

" There was a certain hermit, a companion of
St. Anthony of Egypt, who, for sixty years, had
remained in the desert, engaged in the contemplation of the perfections of the everlasting Creator.
To him the world and all its treasures were as
nothing; for he thought only of the life to come.

" For sixty years had this pious man continued
in the daily performance of his religious duties,

fasting and praying with rigid regularity, when it pleased Providence to put his faith to the proof, by subjecting him to powerful temptation.

"One day, as he was wandering over the desert, he was assailed by an evil spirit, who seizing him, kept him in his grasp, so that he had no rest from his torment and anguish day or night. Having sought relief in vain, he asked the demon many things; and amongst others, why he and his associates were ever seeking occasion to torment and injure the human race.

"'Our motive,' replied the fiend, 'is jealousy, our motive is envy; for are we not fallen irrevocably? Who shall save us from our eternal doom? To man the Almighty has granted the power to accomplish his own salvation. The unspeakable blessings of heaven are within the reach of every son of Adam, if he will but seek to obtain them. Therefore it is, that we would fain make mankind even as ourselves; therefore it is, that we lose no opportunity of torturing them into an abandonment of their faith, that they may curse God and die.'

"The hermit, upon this, questioned the fiend touching the mansions of bliss in heaven, and begged him to describe the effect produced upon

him by them. 'No description, no words,' replied
the foul spirit, 'can serve to convey the most
distant idea of the glories which I there beheld.
The keenest enjoyments of sense, the most ecstatic
pleasures, spiritual and temporal, are as torments,
compared with the sensations felt in that blessed
abode; in comparison with which the greatest
beauty of this world is hideous deformity, and its
sweets gall and wormwood.'

" Then the hermit asked the evil spirit what he
would give to return once more to his former state
of happiness? To which the demon answered, that
he would gladly suffer all the torments inflicted on
mankind since the creation of the world to that
hour, and all the torments of the damned, so that
he might revisit those regions of glory, where the
paths were as refined gold, and the walls as the
emeralds and diamonds of Golconda; in comparison with the brightness of which the noon-day
sun, with the moon and all the stars, are as the
darkness of death; where there is no weariness
of body nor tribulation of spirit, and hunger and
thirst are unknown.

" Whereupon the good hermit shook from him
the evil spirit, saying, 'What are the pains and

troubles of this life, if their reward be such as I have just heard? who would not cheerfully encounter all the ills of the world—the hatred, the malice, and the persecution of man, nay, the temptation of the evil one, if by so doing he may finally meet acceptance in heaven? My soul is clad with the armour of faith; I will not longer fear the assaults of mine enemies.'—And thereupon he went forth upon his way."

The women listened with evident wonder, and the most profound attention, to the legend; for anything in the shape of a story seldom fails to attract the mind of an Arab. Some of them were evidently moved, and appeared desirous of imitating the example of the good hermit. One of them, with a simplicity at which I could not help smiling, asked me whether there were any camels in the happy regions concerning which I had just been reading? " Because," said she, " how is it possible that we should live without camel's milk? and yet, was it not said that thirst never entered there?" I was rather puzzled how to solve this difficulty; but I told her, that as all that the heart could wish for would be found there, camel's milk, without doubt, would not be wanting.

Finding them in an attentive mood, I then proceeded to read them a chapter from the Gospel, to which also they paid a marked attention : and I would fain cherish the hope, that the thoughts of some of these simple-minded creatures were turned by these humble efforts of mine to the worship of the only true God.

CHAPTER IX.

A Pilgrimage to the Holy Land—A Caravan crossing the Desert—Bagdad—A Chaldean Bishop—A City of Tents—The Valley of the Euphrates—Extraordinary Sagacity of the Camel—A Storm in the Desert—The Ruins of Palmyra—The Valley of the Tombs—Scriptural Traditions.

I HAD long cherished an anxious desire to visit the scenes of the events recorded in holy writ. From a very early age, ever since I was ten years old, I had burned to climb those awful mountains, whence the Creator made known his will to man ; and to behold the desert spot, where the Redeemer of the world fed thousands with five loaves and two small fishes; the scene of the Passion and the Crucifixion for the redemption of man. Often did I dream that I was wandering in those very places, which my soul had so long yearned to visit, until at last I became thoroughly absorbed in this one idea, to the exclusion of nearly every other.

I had passed my time in great contentment amongst my kind and hospitable entertainers; and had it not been for the utter spiritual destitution and constraint in which a due consideration for their prejudices compelled me in a manner to live, I have no doubt that I could have ended my days with them in peace. How many calamities might have been spared me, had such been my lot, God only knows; and I fear that the spiritual advantages which I have attained, by quitting these kind untaught children of nature, in search of virtue in the abodes of Christian civilization, have hardly been commensurate with my sanguine expectations.

Often had I besought my dear father to undertake with me this pious pilgrimage, and I have no doubt that my wishes would have been gratified, if the ruthless hand of blind fanatacism had not closed in death the eyes which longed to gaze with awe on those sacred spots, and silenced the tongue which would have sent forth words of thanksgiving and praise to the Redeemer for his mercy vouchsafed to man.

Since, however, it had pleased the great Disposer of events to deny me the happiness of performing

it in the society of my lost parent, I determined
to fulfil my long cherished journey alone, and to
abandon the land of my forefathers: a land stained
with the blood of one dearer to me than life, and
the rulers of which had made his home a desolation, and his child a wretched outcast on the wide
world.

Before I bade adieu to my kind friends, I
strayed out, to wander again amidst the mouldering ruins of the once mighty Babylon, " Glorious
among kingdoms, the famous pride of the Chaldeans;" that city so great among the nations of
the earth.

As I retraced my steps to the encampment,
through the shapeless mounds and broken pottery
all that now remained of the queen of cities, I
finally made up my mind to quit the tent of my
kind host, the Sheikh Dryaah Ebn Shalan, and
bend my steps towards Palestine, as I best might,
placing my trust in that Great Being who had
already so often preserved me in many a deadly
trial.

Full of this determination, I no sooner gained
the encampment than I went straight to the tent
of the good-hearted chief, to announce my inten-

tion. The sheikh expressed his regret that I
should have resolved on leaving them so soon:
adding, however, that if my destiny required me
to go, opposition was of course out of the question.
I had even more difficulty in reconciling myself
to part with my Bedouin female friends, whose
simple and unaffected behaviour towards me had
entirely won my affection, and made a separation
from them little less severe than a parting from
beloved friends and kindred.

At last, after regrets and lamentations, mingled
with hopes that we might meet again ere long, I
tore myself from them, after having resided with
them six months, and departed for Bagdad, in
search of the next caravan journeying to Damascus,
accompanied with the warmest wishes for my safety
and welfare, and the most eloquent benedictions
their glowing hearts could shower upon my head.
The chief kindly offered to give me an escort to
Bagdad, but I did not think myself justified in
profiting by his goodness.

Farewell, simple-hearted children of the Desert!
In bidding you adieu, how little did I think I was
leaving behind me so many virtues, which I was not
destined to meet with in your more civilized fellow

men! In the virtues of hospitality and charity, what people can equal you? In the sacred duties of friendship, who can surpass you? True, you are robbers—you are slayers of men, and for this end you say you were born; this you assert to be a privilege bestowed on you, through your great father Ismael, by the Almighty himself. Oh, that it would please Him, to add to your dauntless courage, your powers of patient endurance, your excellent friendship, your generous hospitality, your boundless charity, your almost spotless chastity, the still higher virtues of Christian piety! Then would you excel all living men, from north to south, and from the rising to the going down of the sun!

Upon my arrival at Bagdad, I learned that a caravan, consisting of an immense number of travellers, of every nation and calling, had been collecting for the last seven or eight months, the roads being, during the whole of that time, so infested by robbers, that it was impossible to proceed with safety, and would start in the following month of March, for Damascus. By this caravan, therefore, I determined to proceed to Palestine.

Amongst those who, like myself, were awaiting the departure of the caravan, was a Christian bishop, named Deir Stefan, from the regions of Tartary, near the Caucasus, about forty-five years of age, an old friend of my father's, who was also about to make a pilgrimage to the Holy Land. Hearing that he intended to make the same journey as myself, I proposed to him that we should travel together, to which he readily assented. With this pious man and a lady who had come to join the caravan from Bassorah, with two children and many slaves, I united myself, and we soon became a most harmonious little family, for the lady was also a Chaldean Christian. I never had the good fortune to meet with a man possessing more true piety, than this bishop, nor one more fitted to fill his sacred office, both with learning and zeal. I fancied I perceived in him a resemblance to my poor father; and this, doubtless, possessed me strongly in his favour. I believe he is still living, and, with the grace of God, I hope I may be again permitted to behold his face.

The multitude were encamped in a vast plain, about an hour and a half distant from the city. I am sure I do not exaggerate when I estimate the camels and horses belonging to the caravan at fifteen thousand; so great was the number of travellers, swelled by a prodigious quantity of hadjis, or pilgrims, of all denominations, both Mahomedan and Christian.

Every day brought fresh arrivals; crowds flowing in from all quarters. Sometimes whole families of pilgrims joined our caravan at a time; which was also constantly augmented by traders proceeding to Damascus, and different parts of Syria; Persians, Osmanli Turks, and merchants from Bassorah. For ten days the arrivals were incessant; and nothing could be more interesting than the sight of so many men assembled together, differing so widely in language, manners, and dress. Many and many a heart-moving scene did I then behold; —parents taking leave of children, and children of parents; wives, with their faces bathed in tears, bidding adieu to their husbands, who were about to brave the dangers of the desert, perchance never more to return to their arms.

For me, alas! there were none to weep. I was alone, and there was no one to utter a benediction on my head. How bitterly did I feel my lonely state ! for my goings and comings were unheeded as the course of the date leaf, which is blown here and there over the wild desert, and no man takes account of it. How are the springs of my soul dried up ! The cup of my affections is empty.

I turned my thoughts to Heaven, and lifting my prayer to the Giver of all good things, besought Him to shield me, his unhappy daughter, bereft of friend and protector, from the dangers of the desert—from the deadly samiri, and from the assaults of the robber and the homicide. I put up a prayer to my beloved father to intercede for me at the throne of grace, that I might escape those dangers, and obtain pardon for my sins and transgressions.

The time fixed for our departure was approaching. Our vast encampment teemed with provisions and stores for the journey; every one laying in a supply sufficient for two or three months, as if we had been about to embark on ship-board : for, in truth, the prospect of procuring fresh supplies was not more promising, than in the case of a vessel about to cross the ocean. Camel load, after camel load, poured into the camp, consisting of flour biscuit, and rice ; besides quantities of " basterma," a kind of sausage, which is dried, and keeps well for a considerable length of time; " kaourma," a preparation of hashed beef or mutton, cooked in grease and crammed into skins, which is dished up, during the journey, with dates and herbs, and makes a very palatable dish; " halawah," a sweet solid substance, composed of the " simsim," described in my account of the manufactures of Telkef, honey, and other ingredients. In addition to these, piles of carpets, cushions, and bed-clothes, were to be seen on every side, together with a prodigious quantity of kitchen utensils of every description. The bishop, the Bassorah lady, and myself, occupied but one tent; which, as usual, was separated in the middle by a curtain, the gentleman being on one side, and the ladies on the other.

Although our caravan was furnished with so great a number of camels, the travellers, including pilgrims, merchants, camel-drivers, attendants, and escort, did not amount to more than five thousand individuals; a very large proportion of the camels being destined to carry merchandize, of which there was an immense quantity. Besides this, no inconsiderable number were required for the purpose of conveying the tents, baggage, and provisions of the travellers. My fellow-traveller, the bishop, had five camels for his own use and that of his attendants. I had the same number; but our companion from Bassorah had no fewer than fifteen, for the use of herself, children, and servants.

It must not be supposed that these camels were the property of the individual travellers. There is a class of men who gain their livelihood by letting out these animals for hire, with whom a bargain is made by the persons about to proceed on a journey, at a certain price; the proprietor of the camels undertaking to load, unload, and feed them during the whole time, besides providing drivers to attend them.

I think I paid at the rate of about three hundred piastres for each camel; and this included everything, so that I had no further trouble about the matter. Every morning at day-break I found my beasts all loaded, and one saddled for my own personal service; and certainly, nothing could exceed the assiduity and punctuality with which the duties connected with this service were performed in every particular. Besides my little

troop of camels, I had a horse for riding, which
enabled me to vary the slow monotonous pace of
the caravan with an occasional gallop over the
desert. This horse I often lent to my reverend
companion, who was very grateful for the trifling
attention.

At last the day of departure arrived, and at early
dawn we set out on our long march, leaving behind
us a sorrowing crowd of the friends and relations
of our fellow-travellers, who stood gazing at our
almost interminable file of animated beings, as it
struggled along with tardy pace, looking like a
gigantic snake writhing its way over the wide-
stretching plain before it,—mingling benedictions
and prayers for our safety with their parting tears.

Onward the living mass bent its course; the
camels, with grave demeanour, like well-drilled
soldiers, keeping their file with a strictness which
would win the approbation even of a European
drill-serjeant; those destined to carry the travellers
having strapped on their backs maharahs of every
colour, from lively red to deep purple, from emerald green to deep blue, each holding six persons,
and presenting the appearance of a moving city
of brilliant coloured houses. The escort of cavalry

furnished by the Pasha of Bagdad, who were nearly all Georgians, and afforded a striking contrast, by the fairness of their complexions, with the swarthy visaged multitude with whose protection they were charged, rode before and behind.

The camel-drivers walked by the side of their charge, and the whole caravan—composed of this motley group of baggage camels, riding camels, camels laden with merchandize, horses, cavalry, pilgrims, rich and poor, some mounted on camels, and others, less fortunate, walking on foot, drivers, slaves, flocks of sheep, with their owners, who had joined the caravan for the purpose of selling them to the travellers in the course of the journey, and, if I recollect rightly, a few bullocks—forming a line not less I am sure than a mile in length, proceeded continually onward for ten hours, when a halt was made. During our march we aroused whole herds of gazelles, who fled in all directions, in great trepidation, over the plain.

The rapidity with which the camels were un-laden and the tents pitched is perfectly incredible. In less than half an hour a vast city of tents arises, as if by the touch of an enchanter's wand; and

M 2

while the inexperienced traveller surveys with
wonder and admiration the erection of a spacious
square on his right, he suddenly casts his eyes to
the left and finds that a long lane of tents has
sprung up, as it were, out of the bowels of the
earth.   The city, if I may so call it, being thus
built, a rampart is forthwith cast up around it, by
placing the camels, (which had been fed with date
kernels), with their pack-saddles, in a circle, on the
outer verge of the encampment; precautions are
then taken to guard the caravan from sudden
attack, and the travellers begin to think about
their supper.

The travelling butchers were now all on the
alert, and purchases were making in all directions.
Sheep were slaughtered, and every body purchased
according to his wants, the price paid being about
five or six paras for the ratel, or five pounds for five
farthings. The purchase being made, no time was
lost in preparing the meat for table, the cooks fully
equaling the tent builders in expertness and rapidity.
Fires were made on the ground, and immediately
the air was filled with those acceptable hissing
sounds which, after a long fast, are sweeter music

than the voice of his mistress to the sighing lover, and upon hearing which the sternest visage puts on a momentary gleam of benignity.

Before the door of each tent, slaves were seen busily engaged in spreading the large white cloths upon the bare ground ; and it was not long before every cloth was surrounded by a company evidently fully disposed to devote themselves seriously to the business in hand. Before half an hour had passed away, whole sheep had disappeared, and lofty mountains of rice had been laid low; and when the company had had their fill, the servants were permitted to regale themselves on the remains, of which there was an abundance. Our party consisted of twelve, every one of whom appeared bent upon promoting the common comfort. After supper, we remained engaged in converse until eleven o'clock, before which hour it was idle to think of retiring to rest, for the incessant loud laughter, shouts, and clamour of the Georgian guard, calling to each other all over the encampment, made sleep entirely out of the question.

At eleven, however, we spread our carpets and lay down to sleep. I had by this time become so

reconciled to taking my rest upon the ground,
that I slept soundly the whole of the night.   And
to say the truth, my six months' apprenticeship
amongst my Bedouin friends, proved an excellent
preparative for caravan travelling; and I had the
satisfaction of finding that I enjoyed a considerable
advantage, in that respect, over those who had
been dwelling exclusively in cities, seeing that I
was enabled to find comfort and ease where they
could only discover restless annoyance.

   We arose at daybreak, and again set out in the
same order as on the preceding day, without waiting for breakfast; which every one took at his
leisure on the back of his camel.   For this purpose
every animal carries, suspended at his shoulder, a
" khorj," or basket, containing cheese, biscuits,
basterma, eggs, and other provisions, and a skin
filled with water, called " matārah."   Thus the
traveller takes his breakfast; thus he dines, and
not unfrequently sleeps, rarely dismounting from
his camel, until the caravan reaches its halting
place for the night.

   We continued our journey for ten days, during
the whole of which we skirted the fertile bank of

the beautifully-winding Euphrates, cheered by the sight of its fresh green pastures, and fanned by the soft zephyrs of spring; building our city at night, and destroying it in the morning; so that no vestige remained, save the extinct embers of our fires, well-stripped bones, and the refuse of the last night's meal.

At the expiration of that time our road lay to the westward; so that we were compelled to cross the river, and exchange its pleasant bank for the salt and arid desert which lay beyond.   It was at Hid that we crossed the Euphrates; and, as may be well imagined, the passage of so vast a multitude of men and women, beasts and baggage, was not accomplished without considerable delay as well as danger.   For two days the ferry boats were constantly occupied in transporting the mingled crowd across the stream, although an immense number were employed in the service.

In order to prevent the camels from struggling during the passage, the effect of which would be, in all probability, to swamp the boat, the animals are secured by the right fore leg; by which means, and the soothing exhortations of their drivers, the sagacious creatures are conveyed across in safety.

There is a song sung by the drivers, which appears
to produce a surprising effect upon them, rendering them perfectly quiet and docile. It begins
with the words "Shekh shillunu."—"Lend a
hand to the old."

The boat in which I crossed over was, for some
time, in no small danger of being upset. My
friends and myself, together with our servants, a
great number of camels, and a heavy weight of
baggage, were all crammed into one boat, of a size
altogether inadequate to the passage of so great a
load, and our gunwale was within a few inches of
the water. As it eddied round in the stream,
with an unsteady, oscillating motion, I expected to
see the water rush in on one side or the other; and
alarm was depicted upon every countenance, when
one of the animals, more frightened than the rest,
contrived, by a violent effort, to disengage its leg
from the cord by which it was fastened, and, by
its uneasy starts, greatly increased our danger.
Besides which, the terrific cries of the affrighted
animals added to the terrors of our situation.

I must confess I felt seriously alarmed, as I saw
our bark driving down the stream far below the
landing-place, and apparently utterly baffling the

strength of the boatmen, who tried in vain to
direct its course. I had fully made up my mind
that, at the very least, we could not have escaped
without a severe wetting, when the boat, more, I
believe, from the direction given to it by a cross
current, than any skill on the part of the boatmen,
drove ashore, at the distance of about half an hour's
walk from the point at which we were to have
landed. The moment I set my foot in the little
town of Hid, I returned thanks to Almighty God
for what I could only consider as a miraculous
preservation.

Wearied with fatigue and anxiety, the exhausted
travellers set about preparing their evening meal;
after which, we were all too happy to retire to
rest, after the toils and perils of the day. Next
morning we rose, as usual, at daybreak, and prepared to quit the Euphrates; not without sensations of regret, for we felt that we were taking
leave of a kind friend, whose smiling face had
beguiled and cheered us on our weary way.

We were now about to cross a salt desert tract
of vast extent. The ground was white with saline
particles, and the whole prospect before us was as
dreary and desolate as the imagination can well

conceive. As it was a matter of certainty that no opportunity would present itself, for a long time to come, of laying in a supply of water and provisions, we were constantly engaged during the two days occupied by the transit of the caravan, in providing ourselves with the necessary stores, and filling the water skins from the Euphrates. I was very fortunate in my foraging expedition, and quite astonished my fellow-travellers by the quantity of chickens, eggs, and other little matters, which I had succeeded in purchasing at Hid.

We now proceeded on our way across the desert. Hour after hour, as we wended on our dreary course, not a patch of verdure was to be seen in any direction. The weary eye strained in vain to catch any object that might relieve the tiresome monotony; as far as sight could reach the plain was level as the surface of a lake, with an horizon exactly like that of the ocean, without the slightest undulation of outline. The only relief to the scene was when some wild animal, scared by the approach of so vast a multitude, was seen to gallop off in the distance. They never came sufficiently near us to enable me to distinguish their exact form; but I was told by an older traveller than myself, that they were lions. Track there was none; and we kept our course by the compass and the stars.

In journeys of this description, every person's camel may be considered as his ship, fully victualled and stored, so that no article of necessity shall be found wanting. Nothing can be more comfortable than the saddles, either for sitting or lying upon. Upon them at least two meals are taken during the day; for the caravan always starts at daybreak, and no time is allowed for breakfast; which, as well as dinner, is, as I have already said, taken on the road. Neither is this mode so inconvenient or disagreeable as might be imagined; for the pace of the camel is as gentle as the rocking of an infant's cradle. Besides this, the necessity imposed on every traveller of taking these two meals in comparative solitude, gives an additional zest to the social assemblage at supper, when the caravan halts for the night.

I passed the greater part of my time in reading; but often, as the day advanced, the heat, combined with the gentle see-saw motion of the camel's pace, rendered sleep irresistible. One day, I remember, slumber overtook me while I was reading, and the book dropped from my hand to the ground; upon which, the sagacious camel immediately stopped, and would not proceed until it had been picked up. This is one instance amongst hundreds of the sagacity of this, the most docile, the most submissive to the will of man, and, I believe, the most sagacious animal in the whole creation. It obeys the slightest sign from its master; going down on its knees at a moment's notice, and seeming, in short, to divine the wishes of its lord by a sort of instinct.

On the third day after our departure from Hid, as we were going, as usual, listlessly on, I saw upon a sudden a great commotion towards the front of our cavalcade. I was, of course, anxious to ascertain the reason of so unusual an occurrence, and inquired of a man, whom I saw hurrying past me, with alarm in his countenance, what had happened. " The samiri ! the samiri !" he cried, " is approaching !" " The samiri !" I said to myself, " how can that be? Not a cloud is to be seen; the sky is clear and bright; not a breath of air is stirring. How can this be? by what means have they come at the knowledge that this scourge of the desert is about to pour its fury on our heads?"

I was not suffered to remain long in doubt. The camels in the front rank had, I was told, refused to proceed, which was an infallible sign that the dreaded wind was not far off. Two hours before its approach they seem to scent its coming; for nothing can induce them to continue their onward course. Though upon all other occasions they are the most docile and obedient of living creatures, they become, under these circumstances, more perverse and obstinate than the ass or the mule. They bury their heads in the sand, and remain crouched down, until the scourge has passed over them. This wonderful instinct bestowed on them by the great Creator of all things for their own preservation, is also instrumental in saving the lives of innumerable travellers, who, ignorant of the approach of the wind, would be overwhelmed and suffocated by it, before they could make any efforts for their own preservation.

No sooner was it known that the samiri was near at hand, than a halt was immediately called, and all became bustle and confusion. The tent camels were quickly unloaded, and the tents pitched, with a rapidity increased by fear and dread. The horses were secured, their heads covered and their ears filled with cotton. As for the camels, the faithful harbingers of danger, they were left to their own sagacity.

The travellers had now betaken themselves to their tents, where they cast themselves on the ground, and covered their heads with the "mashallah." A profound stillness reigned throughout the vast multitude, as if every one expected to escape the fury of the blast, by keeping his very existence a secret.

Still the samiri came not. An hour had passed away, and the sky was yet serene, and the air tranquil. When the intelligence which had thrown us into this state of consternation was first brought to us, a Turkish lady, who was travelling with us, happened to be near me. This lady seemed disposed to laugh at the fears expressed by more experienced travellers. After giving orders for the pitching of her tent, she invited me to join her in a cup of coffee and a chibouk, saying that she was certain the samiri would not reach us for some time to come; perhaps not for an hour or more. From the continued fineness of the weather, and the stillness of the atmosphere, I was much disposed to be of her way of thinking, and accepted her invitation with pleasure, as an agreeable mode of passing the time until the approach of the wind should warn me to fly to my tent.

As I lifted the curtain of it, I thought I perceived a slight motion in the air, but I took no heed of it, and was soon comfortably seated with my Turkish acquaintance, talking over indifferent matters, sipping some excellent coffee, which her slaves had prepared at a very short notice, and enjoying my chibouk. It was, however, not long before I saw the sides of the tent agitated, slightly at first, but gradually increasing in violence. I rose hastily from my cushion, and putting aside the curtain, looked out upon the desert.

Casting my eyes to windward, I beheld a vast column, which seemed to reach from earth to heaven, gradually approaching our encampment. Round and round the huge lurid mass whirled, as it slowly but steadily kept its onward progress, casting a deep shadow across the naked desert. Above my head all was serenity and peace; but, as the column approached, the gusts which had just now produced the slight rustling in the curtains of the Mahomedan lady's tent, became more sudden and violent; now chilling the blood, and now scorching, like the blast of a furnace.

I felt a sensation of terror creeping over me; my strength seemed to have abandoned my limbs; I felt as though I was suffocated, and gasped for breath. All hopes of gaining my own tent were vain, for the samiri was now at hand. I closed the curtain in haste, and, stretching myself on the ground, covered my head and face with my " mashallah." My companion did the same, and we awaited the passage of the scourge in silent dread.

The sides of our tent were now shaken with fearful violence. I expected every moment to see it lifted high in the air, and ourselves exposed to the destructive fury of the blast; which makes a speedy tomb for all who oppose its onward progress. The tent was become like a hot bath, and we breathed with the greatest difficulty. I remember well the horror with which, in that moment of terror, I contemplated the idea of dying in the company of an unbeliever. I have lived to entertain more charitable sentiments.

The storm lasted seven or eight hours, at the

end of which we rose from the ground, and, after
returning thanks to Almighty God for our preservation, each after her own fashion, I went forth
from the tent to see what had been the fate of my
own friends. As I passed along the encampment
I met crowds looking like men arisen from the
dead, issuing from their tents, and exchanging
congratulations upon their recent escape; and
turning leeward I beheld the deadly dreaded
column holding on its desolating course towards
the horizon.

The tents being now struck, and the camels
loaded, we proceeded on our way. In our progress we beheld, with horror, the dead bodies of
several Arabs, who had been overtaken by the
samiri, scorched to a cinder on the dreary
waste.

For several days after this awful visitation we
marched on without meeting with any incident
of sufficient moment to break the monotony of the
journey. We had been eight days without seeing
water, and during the whole of that time our poor
camels had not tasted a single drop. Upon the
ninth day they were observed to prick up their ears
and snuff the air, with other demonstrations of rest-

lessness and excitement. On a sudden they began
to utter the most extraordinary cries, stamping
and fidgetting in a way which made it almost
impossible to manage them and retain one's seat.
At length, with one accord, they all made a rush
forward, and started off at a pace of which no one
who has not seen a thirsty camel, which scents
the water, can have any idea. At first I could
not understand this movement; for, look where I
would, no water was perceptible by the eye.

As I had taken care to select one of the tallest
camels I could meet with, in order to have a
better view of the country through which our
path lay, I was now, the first in this involun-
tary camel race, and expected, every moment, to
be dashed to the earth. And, sure enough, we at
last came to the bank of a stream, into which my
camel, altogether forgetful of its accustomed politeness, forthwith plunged up to its middle, and began
to drink eagerly.

If I found it difficult to maintain my seat when
only the animal and myself had the water to ourselves, I now found it next to impossible to do so,
when every minute another and another camel
dashed in, and what with their plunging and

jostling, I consider it little short of a miracle that I escaped drowning. In this desperate extremity I cried aloud to the driver, whom I saw, looking on with the utmost indifference, at the edge of the bank, to come to my assistance. " Come and save me," I said; " if you do not, I and your camel must both sink together."

" Fear nothing," he replied, " the camel is wise; Allah has given him knowledge that he may not perish in the water." " That may be very true," I rejoined, " but how is it possible that he can know the depth of this stream, in which, most probably, he never was before?" " By the beard of my father, by the light of my eyes," continued he, " you are safe: on my head be it. Which of the dangers of the desert has Providence hidden from the holy animal?"

This calm resignation to the will of destiny, when the danger is another's, I could readily understand; but, notwithstanding his assurances, I felt no little alarm at my perilous position, from which I saw no means of extricating myself. However, as the driver refused to lend me any assistance, and seemed resolved to leave the result to Providence, I could only resign my fate into his hands.

When the camels had drunk their fill they walked out in the calmest manner imaginable, with their bellies swelled to the size of mountains. We then proceeded to unload our beasts and pitch our tents; for we had determined to pass the night at this refreshing spot; where I enjoyed a delightful walk along the banks of the stream before supper.

On the next day we were so unfortunate as to fall in with a predatory tribe, the name of which I did not learn, though I have every reason to believe that they formed a part of the great Anazi family. On taking measure of their force, it was found to be so overwhelming, that resistance would have been sheer folly, and a culpable waste of blood. All idea of hostile proceedings, therefore, having been abandoned, we immediately took the opposite course, and began to show their chiefs the greatest courtesy and respect; for there is no middle way of treating these self-constituted tax-gatherers. If you cannot cut their throats, you must all but lick the dust off their shoes.

I must, however, on the present occasion, do our unwelcome visitors the justice to say, that they were by no means so unreasonable in their ex-

actions as many of the followers of the same profession. The first thing to be settled was, of course,
the proportion of the contribution which each
individual was to pay; and it cannot be denied
that the assessment was made with a scrupulous
regard to the means of the individual, so far as
they could be ascertained; for this was not
always a very easy matter. Many who had been
heard, not many hours before, to boast of their
wealth, now altered their tone. The abject
poverty which had suddenly overtaken them was
truly marvellous.

As well as I can recollect, my share of the
assessment amounted to about a hundred and fifty
piastres, between three and four pounds sterling;
which I did not consider exorbitant, as I had, at that
very moment, hanging at my saddle, a bag containing pearls and jewels to a large amount, which I
was carrying to a merchant, a native of Bagdad
established at Damascus, at the instance of a
common friend.

The Bedouins are, in fact, the actual rulers in
these regions; for it is a farce to say that the
sultan reigns where he is unable to exercise his
authority, and where his own caravans have some-

times been despoiled by the unceremonious Wahabis, of the rich offerings sent by him to ornament the tomb of the prophet at Mecca. They are the lords of the soil, and therefore consider themselves entitled to the tribute, equally with any other sovereign power, although they may not collect it *selon les règles*.

This mighty business being despatched, the plunderers and the party plundered sat down to a copious feast, at the expense of the caravan. Instead of wailings and lamentations for the loss of property, nothing was heard but sounds of revelry and mirth, and the festivities were kept up till a late hour. The following morning, having returned thanks to Providence for our deliverance, we proceeded on our way.

Up to this time I had enjoyed an excellent state of health, and had not suffered in the slightest degree from the fatigue of constant travel. I now, however, fell ill. A few days after our rencontre with the wandering tribe, I suffered from a derangement of the stomach, which gradually increased in violence, until I began to entertain fears that I was destined to perish in the desert, without beholding those holy places which I had so ardently longed to see before I bade adieu to this world.

My illness, I have no doubt, arose from drinking the water, which had been so long in the skins, that it had become slightly putrid. These skins are generally prepared for use by leaving inside them, for a few days, bits of pomegranate skin steeped in water, which are supposed to counteract the disagreeable flavour which would otherwise be communicated by the bladder. Upon this occasion, the skins out of which I was supplied had not been sufficiently prepared by this process; and to this cause I have very little doubt that the decomposition of the water was to be attributed.

However this might be, my illness rapidly increased; my strength failed me; I was tormented by a violent head-ache, and consumed by fever. I was at last altogether unable to quit my camel during the day, and was forced to retire to bed as soon as we halted for the night. As I became weaker and weaker, I gradually abandoned all hopes of recovery, and began to prepare my mind for the great and awful change which, I doubted not, I was shortly to undergo. I resigned my soul to the will of my Creator; for where else could my hope be? I sent for my kind friend, the bishop, and besought him to administer to me those sacraments and consolations, which the priest of our Lord can alone administer to the dying Catholic. He responded to my call with true Christian zeal, and, with the tenderness of a father, prepared to watch the flight of my departing spirit. I confessed, and made my will, giving whatever I possessed to the poor, and appointing him my executor.

We were now drawing near to Tadmor, the ancient Palmyra, and I requested my friend, in case I should be overtaken by death before I reached that place, to see me buried there, at the foot of a mountain which I indicated to him. I besought him likewise to place over my grave a monumental stone, with these words — " Here lies the Daughter of Misfortune." I made him promise to pray for my soul, and think of me, in his wanderings amongst those holy precincts where I had fervently hoped to accompany him.

Fifteen years have passed over my head since that time, when I firmly believed that I felt the icy hand of the grim tyrant upon my heart. God

knows how often and how sincerely I have prayed,
during those years of persecution and affliction,
that my existence had closed in the dreary wilder-
ness! Surrounded, as I then was, by pious and
tender friends, I should have yielded up my spirit,
conscious, at least, that I should leave behind me
one heart that would have mourned my loss, and
poured forth fervent prayers for my happiness hereafter. What pinching privations, what bitter dis-
appointments, what heart-breaking humiliations,
should I have been spared! Had it not been for
my firm reliance on the goodness of my Creator,
and my conviction that those whom he loves he
chastens, it is impossible to say to what act of
desperation I might not have been driven.

Many days passed before I was able to quit the
back of my camel. At length, the disorder having
reached its crisis, I began to mend by slow degrees,
and by the time we reached Tadmor, I was sufficiently recovered to mount on horseback, and pass
the day following our arrival in riding, with my
friends, round the widely extended ruins of this
relic of departed grandeur, where Zenobia, the
proud Queen of the East, once flourished, guarded
by her warriors, and counselled by her wise men.

And yet how little did the valour of the one, or the wisdom of the other, avail to save her fair city from the ruthless hand of the destroyer, or herself from the galling chain of the haughty conqueror! for her glory is departed, like the glory of the wisest of kings, who built Palmyra in the desert, and other strong cities in Emath.

The traveller, exhausted with many a weary day's march over the sandy waste, still slakes his thirst, as in the days of Solomon, at its pleasant springs of fresh water, and lingers awhile to enjoy its green fertility, before he again ventures forth into the dreary desert. As in his days, too, the riches of the East still find their way thither, on their passage to more westerly regions; but, instead of reposing under roofs of marble, the traveller now finds no other shelter from the wind of the desert, but the curtain of his tent. Instead of swarming multitudes of civilized men, surrounded by every luxury which wealth could bring from the east, the west, the north, and the south, he meets only with a few miserable Arabs, who derive a scanty and wretched subsistence from a paltry traffic in salt and soda, which they carry on with Damascus.

As we rode along we beheld endless rows of

Corinthian columns, of which order all the buildings seem to have been, with the exception of one,
the Temple of the Sun. This row of pillars extended, I should say, for at least a mile; some of
the columns being in extremely good preservation,
and others fast going to decay. One or two I
noticed in an unfinished state, in very good
preservation, just as they had been left by the
workmen. In many places the foundations of the
houses plainly indicated the width and direction
of the streets. All was silence and desolation.
The palm-trees, from which the city, both in the
age recorded in Scripture and during the supremacy
of Rome, derived its name, are now nowhere to be
seen. The few inhabitants who still haunt the
desolate city, have taken up their quarters in
miserable huts, built within the enclosure of the
once renowned Temple of the Sun, which they
call " elkhāla," the castle.

After spending some time amidst this forest of
columns, which, from their extreme whiteness,
preserved by the purity of the climate, offer a very
pleasing contrast with the sandy waste forming the
back-ground, we went to see the Wadi el Khabour,

or Valley of the Tombs, which is situated outside
the boundary of the ancient city. This was, perhaps, the most interesting part of our excursion.
The tombs are square buildings, of two or three
stories, each of which contains niches for the
reception of dead bodies, and in some of which I
believe mummies have been found, resembling
those discovered in the pyramids of Egypt. In
many of the ceilings of these chambers the paint-
ing is still visible, the designs consisting, for the
most part, of heads painted in compartments of a
diamond shape.

A fountain, surrounded by a pile of huge stones,
was pointed out to us, which we were told had
been constructed by Aurelian, and which the
Arabs, for that reason, call Ain Ornus.

Besides their petty trade in salt and soda, with
the latter of which articles they supply the soap-
makers of Damascus, the inhabitants of Tadmor
do not occupy themselves with labour of any kind.
They neither sow nor till, but depend for the small
supplies necessary for their wants on the sale of
the above-mentioned articles.

The tract through which we had now to pass,

on our way to Damascus, which was distant about
a hundred and forty miles, was as dreary and
desolate as that we had traversed on our way
from Hid to Tadmor. When we had journeyed
two days, a mountain of great length and height
was pointed out to me on the left hand, in the
distance, near which the tribes inhabiting these
desert places firmly believe the true site of the
condemned cities of Sodom and Gomorrha to
have been. There are said to be streams flowing
at the foot of this mountain, the waters of which
produce a most pernicious effect on the human
body. This the Arabs attribute to the curse of the
Almighty, which, they say, still hangs over this
unhallowed spot.

Looking in the direction of this mountain, I
observed that a fog hovered over its summit:
while above our heads, and in every other direction around us, the sky was perfectly clear and
bright. This fog, I was told, never quitted the
accursed region, and was another perpetual symbol
of the divine wrath. I heard it also asserted, with
great confidence, that the pillar of salt into which
Lot's wife was turned, for disobeying the divine

injunction, was still to be seen in this neighbourhood. All this information I received with the
most solemn assurances of its truth; but without
feeling, I must honestly confess, any irresistible
desire kindled within me to verify it by actual
investigation.

CHAPTER X.

Damascus from the Desert—Arrival there—Singular Scene—
The City—A Turkish Bath—The Ladies of Damascus—A
Tale of Sorrow—An Accident—Palace of an Aga—A Grand
Dinner at Damascus—Shopping in the East—A Catastrophe
—The Christians of Damascus.

THE time occupied by caravans in travelling
from Bagdad to Damascus, does not usually
exceed forty days. Owing, however, to our numbers, and the enormous quantity of merchandise
which we carried, the loading and unloading of
which took up a considerable time, we had been
well nigh two months on the road, and were yet,
as it seemed, in the midst of the desert. After
quitting the hills which skirt Palmyra to the northwest, we again emerged into an open sandy plain,
unvaried by tree, verdure, or hill. Still holding
our course in a north-westernly direction, we now
began plainly to discern, in the extreme distance,

a lofty range of mountains, which grew in height and majesty as our distance from them diminished.

At length, on the fourth or fifth day after our departure from Tadmor, as we rose with the early dawn, and prepared to set out on our daily march, the domes and minarets of Damascus were pointed out to us in the far distance, their glittering tops standing in bold relief against the huge towering masses of the Anti-Libanus range of mountains, on whose rugged sides the rising sun had just thrown a mantle of the deepest rose-tint ; a colour so charming, that one who has not beheld it rise in a mountainous country cannot conceive half its beauty. Our hearts beat high with joyful expectation, and a change seemed to come over the whole caravan. Instead of plodding onward jaded and listlessly, wearied in body and depressed in spirit by the monotony of the interminable desert, the tones of cheerful conversation were again heard, and an air of liveliness took place of the drowsy vacuity which had just before been depicted on every countenance.

All eyes were turned in one direction, and eagerly fixed upon the long looked-for city; which, at every step, lost somewhat of its fairy and dream-like air, and put on the sober reality of the dwelling place of man, the scene of every-day wants, the theatre of common-place actions and occupations.

It was three o'clock in the afternoon when we arrived at the spot where our caravan was to make its last halt, at about half an hour's distance from the eastern gate of the city. On our left, far away towards the south, rose the softly swelling heights of the Haouran, girded all around by the green luxuriance of their surrounding valleys, whose rising crops fully bore out the claim of this fertile region to be called "the granary of Damascus." Nothing could be more striking than the contrast presented between the dreary sterile region which we were leaving behind, and the appearance of smiling fertility which we had now before us.

The burial-ground for Christians intervened, between us and the city; which lay scattered out before our view, in the midst of a vast plain surrounded by mountain heights of every shape and character, from the gently swelling hill to the bare and rugged granite peak, clad with eternal snow. The irregular masses of white houses, which under a scorching sun and cloudless sky quite

N 3

dazzled the eye-sight, were relieved by the innumerable domes and cupolas of its mosques, its
churches, and its convents; whilst, at intervals,
lofty minarets of exquisite beauty towered above
all, and traced their graceful outline on the soft-
tinted background of the distant Anti Libanus.

The source of the River Barrada, the ancient
Abana and Pharphar, whose seven channels so
effectually contribute to the fertility of this favoured
spot, could be distinctly traced on our right,
beyond the city, by the deep fringe of trees which
lined its bank; and on every side gardens and
orchards, or rather forests, of olive, palm, fig,
apricot, pomegranate, and orange trees, encompassed "the mole of beauty" on every side, and
covered the vast plain.   From this point the line
of the street, that is called "strait," mentioned in
the Acts of the Apostles, was plainly distinguishable,
by the prominent public buildings lining its course,
—the castle and palace, the principal khan, and
the great mosque, formerly the Christian Church
of St. John.   Between us and the "strait street,"
the Christian quarter intervened, distinguished by
its church tops and convent towers.

On arriving at our encamping ground, we found

a multitude of expectant friends and relatives, who
had pitched their tents of many colours near the
appointed spot, and where they were anxiously
awaiting the arrival of the caravan.   What a scene
of bustle and confusion !   Question upon question
—answer upon answer, with breathless rapidity !
Every body talking at the same time, and all in a
state of enthusiastic delight: some at finding their
friends in safety, on whose behalf they had suffered
no small anxiety and alarm ; others from the hardly
less satisfaction at finding that their merchandise
had escaped the unceremonious grasp of Bedouin
fingers.   Every hour brought fresh arrivals at our
encampment, and added to the din of conversation,
on which all were eager to speak, and none to listen.

We travellers had now a weighty business to
despatch, namely, the settlement of our accounts
with the owners of the camels, supplied for our use
during the journey.   This business over, we proceeded to make preparations for a grand farewell
feast, in which the travellers and their friends
purposed to celebrate their happy meeting.

I was met by a rich merchant of Damascus,
named El Hawaja Yusuf Hanhowri, to whom I

had brought letters of recommendation. He brought with him his children and his brother; and, after making us an offer of his services, politely pressed us to make use of his house as our home, until we could settle ourselves at Damascus; a proposition to which we gladly and thankfully assented.

That night we slept, for the last time, in our tents; and upon the following morning I left the encampment, with my travelling companion the bishop, the Bassorah lady with her family, and Yusuf Hanhowri, and made my entry into " Sham El Sherifa,"—" Damascus the noble;" " Ferdos El Arthee,"—" the Paradise of the Earth." On reaching the eastern gate, from a loop-hole in which it is said St. Paul was let down in a basket, and thus escaped the fury of the enraged Jews, we met with a serious difficulty. In Damascus, as in many other Oriental cities, no Christian is permitted to enter upon horseback. Being rather indisposed, I was mounted on the mare which I had brought with me, and the guards at the gate distinguishing us, I suppose, by our particular dress and that of the bishop, to be Christians, resolutely refused us permission to enter, unless I dismounted.

A great deal of quarrelling ensued; for my

friend Yusuf Hanhowri, a person of consideration
and influence, and well known to the Pasha, filled
with indignation to think that any one under his
protection should be subject to detention and
insult, entered into a warm altercation with the
guard. For a long time all his remonstrances and
threats were unavailing; until a message was conveyed from Yusuf to the commander of the troops,
which quickly brought the required permission,
and I was allowed to pass the gate without molestation. We all took up our quarters in the house
of the hospitable Yusuf, until we could find a
suitable habitation; and during our stay with him
we received constant proofs of his kindness of
disposition and unaffected goodness of heart.

The day after my arrival, the wife of my host
proposed that we should go together to the " hammām," or bath; an offer which I accepted with
great thankfulness; for to one who, like myself,
had been accustomed from childhood to resort to
this luxury at least twice a week, a two months'
deprivation had proved inconceivably irksome and
annoying. We were ten in number, and took with
us ten slaves. My travelling companion from
Bassorah and her daughter accompanied us.

The bath to which we went was one of the most
splendid in Damascus, so famous for its public
baths. The walls of the saloon were all of polished
marble; the floor was of the same material, cu-
riously wrought into the most beautiful mosaics,
and shone like a mirror. The ceiling was in the
form of a dome, and was covered with glazed tiles
of beautiful and brilliant coloured glass of every
hue. There were many other bathing rooms in
the establishment; but this was the largest of all.
Upon entering it, we found two hundred females, all
in a state of nudity, with the exception of an apron
of white silk, with stripes of red or some other gay
colour, descending to the knees. Some were undergoing the operation of bathing; some smoking
their nerghilahs; others, reclining on diwans,
taking refreshment; while here and there were
seen groups of as beautiful forms as ever sculptor
chiselled, engaged in conversation, which, judging
from the bursts of laughter which it seemed to
provoke, appeared to be of a lively nature.

The process of bathing was similar to that prevailing in the generality of eastern cities. All
round the walls of the saloon, cocks are placed at
intervals, which furnish a constant supply of warm

and cold water. Under each pair is fixed a marble basin or vase, mounted on a pedestal, of beautiful form and workmanship, about two feet high, and the same in diameter.

The bather is placed on a low wooden stool raised about a foot from the ground, and the " rhasalat," or bathing woman, (one of whom stands in front and pours warm water over the head and body, whilst another, stationed behind the bather, proceeds to rub over her head and on the surface of her skin, an earth brought from Aleppo, called "gil" in the Chaldean tongue, mixed with sweet-scented herbs,) begin their operations. This earth is kept in a basin, into which hot water is poured when the operator is about to use it, and possesses the quality of cleansing and purifying the skin, besides rendering its surface smooth and soft like silk. When this has been strongly rubbed over the head and body for about two or three minutes, it is washed off with warm water; which is handed, as often as it is required, by another attendant. Vase after vase of warm water is now poured over the bather, who is afterwards covered with a lather, made of soap scented with a thousand odours. To this a second deluging with warm water suc-

ceeds. The skin is then dried, and afterwards
rubbed with a bag composed of a white substance,
made of the fibres of a plant called " leef," which
is rough and, produces somewhat the effect of a
horse-hair glove, in promoting a general warmth
and grateful excitement on the surface of the body.
The soles of the feet are rubbed, or rather polished,
with a piece of smooth pumice stone, which is
fixed in a handle generally of metal, but frequently
of gold or silver.

This operation, which, though long, is nevertheless extremely agreeable, very often lasts for an
hour; after which some of the bathers stretch
themselves on the diwans, or couches, around the
ante-chamber; others lie along on the polished
marble pavement, and enjoy their sherbet, their
coffee, and their nerghilahs; whilst their slaves
and attendants minister to them the most varied
and exquisite perfumery, which their plains, so
rich in flowers of the sweetest odour, can supply.

Such a chattering I think my ears never before
endured. It was enough to bewilder the brain;
for the public baths of Damascus are the scandal
markets of that populous city. Here it is that the
fair Damascenes settle the pretensions of their

rivals, and circulate their little elegant slanders. Here, they not unfrequently spend nearly the entire day, in bathing, eating, drinking their sherbet, smoking their nerghilahs, talking, and even dancing. For this pastime negresses are employed, who maintain the dance almost incessantly; each lady getting up and joining in her turn, and sitting down again, when fatigued with the exercise.

As I was a stranger amongst them, of course their curiosity was raised to a high pitch to know who and what I was; and I had no sooner finished my bath than I was surrounded by a host of my fair fellow bathers, and assailed with a thousand questions, which it would have taken me a week to answer truly and satisfactorily. I told them that I was from Bagdad; and they thereupon stunned me with a multitude of inquiries respecting the ladies of that city; how they dressed, how they looked, what were their amusements, were they short or tall, fair or dark, lean or plump, and an infinity of similar questions respecting their habits and appearance, and the treatment they received from their lords;—all which I answered as well and as briefly as I could.

There was one among them, fairer than her companions, on whose countenance I observed a change as I pronounced the word Bagdad. Her cheek was instantly suffused with a flush, her lips trembled, and I thought I saw a tear standing in her eye.

When I had, in some degree, succeeded in allaying the thirst for information which seemed to burn in the breasts of the Damascus belles, on turning my head round, I observed that the lady on whose countenance I had just seen so sudden a change produced, had placed herself by my side, and was regarding me with fixed attention and anxiety.

" You are from Bagdad," she whispered in my ear.

" I am," I replied, wondering what was to come next.

" Alas!" she exclaimed, with visibly increasing agitation, " I, too, am from that city. May I entreat a moment's conversation."

" Bismillah," I replied. Upon which she led the way into another apartment, adjoining the saloon where this conversation had passed, in which was situated the plunging and swimming bath, inviting me aloud, as we quitted the room, in order that our going out might not attract attention, to try my prowess in swimming against hers.

We were no sooner alone than she burst into a flood of tears, and some time elapsed before she became sufficiently calm to utter a word. I tried every thing in my power to console her, and, with all the gentleness I was mistress of, I besought her to pour into my ear the cause of her bitter grief, that I might share the load which pressed upon her heart.

" Alas !" she cried, " how little do you know, lady, the tumult which that single word uttered by you aroused in my breast; for how could you possibly conceive the mingled recollections of past happiness and bitter regret, which that name has awakened ?

" My father was a man of consideration and influence in Bagdad, although he professed the Christian religion. Under his fostering care, I was reared and educated; for my mother perished in bringing me into the world. I had only attained my thirteenth year when death robbed me of my remaining parent, and I was left without friend or protector. During my father's lifetime, we received frequent visits from an opulent Turkish Aga, who professed the most friendly sentiments towards him, and treated me with marked attention and respect. When the usual time for mourning had passed, this Aga renewed his visits, which became more and more frequent, until it was impossible for me to disguise from myself the conviction, that a tender sentiment towards me was the motive which prompted these extraordinary attentions.

" All surmises on that head were shortly after put an end to, by his own declaration, that to possess me was the cherished object of his existence. He exhausted his imagination in lavishing praises on my perfections, which he declared exceeded in number the stars in the firmament. He was liberal to profusion in his offers, and promised me presents that might have tempted an Amira, if I would yield to his wishes. But I was deaf to his entreaties. I could not contemplate without feelings of horror the idea of passing the rest of my days as the companion of a man who denied the truth of the religion in which I had been educated, and looked upon its votaries only as dogs. I was ready to suffer a thousand deaths, rather than abandon the faith of my forefathers.

"The enraged Aga, infuriated by my unconquerable obstinacy in refusing an offer which he had looked upon as irresistible, and determined to effect his purpose at all hazards, carried me off by main force, a few days after. Resistance on my part was altogether out of the question. My struggles were unavailing. I fell into a swoon; and, upon my recovery, I found myself in the zenana of my betrayer. Again the Aga renewed his protestations of love; again he laid at my feet presents of matchless rarity and price: nothing could move my inflexible determination. My persecutor was at his wit's ends; for the law of Mahomet forbids the offering of violence to women with the most solemn strictness, and punishes it with the most inflexible rigour.

"In this dilemma, he had recourse to a philtre called "zuhor," which, it is said, has the effect of awakening sentiments of love in obdurate bosoms, towards those who have before inspired no other feeling than that of hatred or dread. With this philtre he so drugged the coffee served to me by his slaves, that, all unconscious of what I was doing, stupefied by the potent charm which he had thus basely administered to me, I was at length induced to consent to our union, which was forthwith solemnized, and—I sink into the earth as I say it—to abjure my religion.

" All this took place in the space of forty hours, during which the deadly drug that I had swallowed maintained its power. When my senses returned, it seemed as if I had been awakened from some hideous dream, and I was about to offer up a fervent prayer to Providence, when the dreadful truth flashed upon me, that to retrace my steps was impossible. For who has ever known the stern, relentless follower of Mahomet, loosen his hold upon his victim, once within his grasp? I was devoted to the prophet, and instant death stared me in the face, if I refused to obey his law. What remained for me, but to vent the grief which consumed my heart in fruitless tears and lamentations? Heaven knows that, while my tongue took part in their impious mummeries, Christianity was in my heart; my conscience never failed to torment me, by its reproof for my outward hypocrisy.

" We soon left Bagdad for Damascus, the abode of the Aga and his family, where we have remained

ever since.   No effort has been spared to remove
the weight of grief which rests on my mind.   The
Aga is unceasing in his attentions; I reign supreme
in his zenana, and my wish is law.   But what can
recompense me for my degrading apostacy? no
tears can wipe away the foul stain which I have
suffered to drop on the whiteness of my soul."

I endeavoured to console her, by telling her to
be of good cheer, and that Providence would
sooner or later remove the sinful load from her
shoulders, and urge her to avow openly that faith,
which I knew she cherished in the recesses of her
heart.

"Imagine," she continued, "the feelings which
possessed me when I heard, but a short time since,
from your lips, that you were from Bagdad, the
spot on which I bade adieu to happiness for ever!
You must have seen, from my agitation, that my
mind was occupied by far other thoughts than
those of the noisy throng of heedless, happy
creatures, whom we left in the other room."

We now joined the crowd in the large saloon,
lest our long absence should rouse curiosity and
excite attention; but not before she extorted from
me a promise that I would pay her a visit.   In vain

I attempted to excuse myself on the score of ill-health; she promised to send her " tahterawan," a ort of sedan chair with curtains hanging round, for me. Well knowing, as I did, the bigoted detestation with which the Damascenes, above all other believers in Islam, regard Christians, and especially those of Bagdad, I pleaded my strong objection to visit at the houses of Mahometans; but I pleaded in vain. My enthusiastic friend assured me that her husband was free from bigotry, and even entertained a particular regard for the followers of my faith. Besides this, she intimated to me, that in her own particular department she reigned supreme, no one presuming to dispute her authority, or contravene her slightest wish.

Finding all my excuses useless, I was obliged to promise her a visit, when she bade me adieu, with a countenance full of serenity, which showed the relief the disclosure of her sad history had afforded her mind, and left the " hammām," attended by ten jairiahs to her tahterawan, in which she proceeded to her palace, followed by a crowd of Mamelukes and eunuchs. On reaching the large saloon I found the ladies enjoying themselves amazingly, and some dancing with great spirit and vivacity.

" Mashallah!" cried one, on seeing me approach, " here comes our friend from Bagdad; let us see the Bagdad step; we are tired of our old figure." " Do! do!" exclaimed twenty voices at once; " in the name of the hundred and forty thousand prophets, let us see it !"

I assured them I was no dancer, and was acquainted with no step whatever, old or new; but they were not to be thus baffled. I was sitting on the marble pavement, quietly enjoying my nerghila, with the full determination not to put my unpractised limbs to any such absurd use for their entertainment; I told them I was altogether out of practice, and moreover wearied with long travel, and weak from the effects of a fever which had attacked me on my way to Damascus. I added, that a long series of misfortunes had entirely broken down my spirits, and that I could not, in short, yield to their entreaties.

These good-humoured, thoughtless creatures, notwithstanding all this, had made up their minds that I should display my accomplishments, and attributed my reluctance to an overweening diffidence. One of them approached me, and threw a chaplet of flowers over my brow; others

sprinkled me all over with the most delicious
perfumes; while two of them, more determined
than the rest, seized me by the arms and lifted me
from the ground.

It was now evident that I could not escape, and
therefore, as the shortest mode of ridding myself
of their importunities, I determined to gratify them
in the best way I could. I endeavoured to recall
to my memory the long forgotten steps which I
had learned in my childhood; but my spirit wandered, and my limbs had forgotten their cunning.
The marble pavement was as slippery as ice, and,
in turning round, I suddenly lost my balance and
fell backwards, dashing my head against the floor
with frightful violence.

What took place immediately afterwards, I only
learned from the lips of those who stood around
me; whose merriment was at once changed to
sorrow and commiseration. From them I learned
that I had no sooner fallen, than I was surrounded
by a pool of blood, which flowed in streams from a
wound in the back of my head. The sorrowing
crowd, who regarded themselves as the cause of
my misfortune, vied with each other in their
humane offices. No time was lost in sending off

a messenger to the neighbouring "aatār," or apo-
thecary; who promptly sent all the necessary
applications: no men being permitted, under any
circumstances, to enter the vestibule of the baths,
whilst females are bathing—any infraction of this
rule being punished with instant death.

For a long time, all their efforts were unavailing
to stop the flow of blood, which continued to defy
all their remedies; so that it was firmly believed
that I must shortly bleed to death. At length,
however, a quantity of burnt camel's hair was
applied to the wound, which promptly stopped the
hemorrhage; after which I was carried into another
apartment and put to bed.

When I came to myself, my brain was on a
whirl. I had no recollection whatever of the
scene which had so lately taken place, and in
which, unfortunately, I had played so prominent
a part. Gradually, however, the facts returned to
my mind, and I became conscious that I was in a
strange room. On raising my eyes, I was overjoyed
to see the countenance of my new acquaintance,
who had, not many hours before, confided to me
her woes and regrets in the plunging room, fair
as the unclouded moon, bending over me with

affectionate anxiety, as though we had been the tenderest of friends from our infancy. I could, in fact, hardly regret the circumstance which had been the occasion of making me acquainted with a heart so tender and affectionate, in the bosom of an utter stranger. I have lived to know and to feel that such are rarely to be found in great civilized cities.

Seeing that I was out of danger, the fair one bade me adieu, and, after exacting from me a renewal of my promise to pay her a visit, as soon as I was sufficiently recovered to go out, she promised to send her own tahterawan to convey me to the house of my friends, and departed.

In a few days after, the tahterawan came, borne by four stout negroes, and conveyed me to the house of Yusuf Hanhowri; where I remained ten days confined to my bed, and during which the Aga's wife sent her slaves to make daily inquiries respecting my progress towards recovery.

In a fortnight, finding myself sufficiently well to venture abroad, I determined to take the earliest opportunity of calling to thank my benefactress for all her kindness. One fine day in May, I left the house of Yusuf Hanhowri, in the Greek quarter of Damascus, accompanied by his

wife and my travelling companion, with the full
intention of redeeming the pledge I had given to
my fair friend; and bent my steps towards the
house of the Aga. Like all the private dwellings
of the most distinguished personages in Damascus,
I found it of very plain exterior, almost approaching
to meanness. The street front presented a black
wall, not unlike that of an European convent,
without any thing to break its naked plainness,
save a very low portal, and a small "shibbak," or
grating, above.

Once, however, inside the gate, and a very
different scene presented itself. I found myself in
the midst of a vast court, paved with marble, and
shaded by tall sycamores and Persian willows;
while numerous fountains, throwing out volumes of
water in an infinite variety of beautiful forms, con-
tributed to set the air in motion, and to counteract
the effect of the sun's burning rays. The walls of
this vast court were covered with vines, arranged
in the form of trellis work. I could not help
detaining the attendants, who were waiting to
conduct me into the presence of my friend, a few
moments, while I admired the beauty of this court,
and the taste displayed in all its arrangements.

I was conducted into a saloon, the furniture of
which surpassed, I think, in richness, all I had
ever before beheld. Here I found my beautiful
friend, who appeared overjoyed to see me so far
recovered; and overwhelmed me with civilities.
She told me that the furniture and decorations of
the room in which we were, cost 150,000 piastres;
and that there were ten or twelve others in the
Aga's palace, equally splendid. Mistress of all
around her, her mind was nevertheless ill at ease.
Christian as she was at heart, she felt that, however
splendid the fetters might be, her body and soul
were alike enslaved. She was not alone when I
entered. Several of the Aga's wives and slaves
were with her; all more or less beautiful, and all
wearing an air of cheerfulness, which contrasted
strongly with the melancholy and pensive ex-
pression, which clouded the brow of my fair
friend.

The length of time during which the wives and
slaves of the more opulent Turks preserve their
good looks and juvenile appearance is truly
remarkable. It is not unfrequently a matter of
no small difficulty to say which is the mother and
which is the daughter; for, in many cases, the

difference in their ages is not more than thirteen
years, and the early period of life at which they
undertake the most serious of the responsibilities of
existence, does not seem to induce, as in other
countries, premature old age,   In fact, the life
they lead mainly contributes to bring about this
result.   From the cradle to the grave, they are
almost exempt from every sort of care ; passing the
even tenour of their lives unruffled by the fastidious
passions, from which the highest are not exempt
in what is here called civilized society.

They pass away their time either in doing
nothing at all, or devote themselves to the acquire-
ment of some accomplishment, such as music,
dancing, or embroidery, and neither know nor
care for what is passing in the world without.
Very few of them are able to read, and the Turk
would disdain to talk of business, or grave matters
of any sort, to a woman.   " Why," ask they,
" should she trouble her head with the details of
a road which she is never destined to travel?"
Besides this, a feeling of jealousy furnishes an
additional motive for keeping them in ignorance.
The zenana, where all that they can desire is
administered to them without stint, and the

"hammām," where they meet their female acquaintances, and enjoy the healthful luxury of bathing, are the whole world to them.

The women of Damascus dress perhaps with more elegance than the females of any other eastern city. They arrange their hair in long tresses, in which are twisted ornaments of gold, pearls, and diamonds. Some of these descend to the ground. I found them full of amiability, and abounding in goodness of heart. Their whole deportment was entirely natural, free from affectation, and full of real kindness and tenderness; and when I look back, and call to mind the serenity and tranquillity of spirit which characterize these illiterate Orientals, and compare it with the condition of those into whose society I have been thrown during my residence in European cities, it has often been with me a question of some doubt, whether the former have any reason to envy the condition of the latter.

The usual complimentary offering of coffee and nerghilahs being over, the Aga's wife pressed me much to stay and dine with her; but I was compelled to decline, having accepted an invitation to pass the day with a friend of Yusuf Hanhowri, a

Christian of the Greek church, who had a beautiful country house, situated to the north of the
city, in the midst of widely extended gardens,
teeming with all the endless variety of delicious
fruits which are found in the fertile plain of
Damascus. He was a man of great wealth and
substance, although he kept the fact as much as
possible a secret from the government; a species
of modest caution which Christians living under
Moslem rule find it extremely convenient to
practice. On bidding my fair friend adieu, I
pledged myself to repeat my visit at the very
earliest opportunity.

The house of my host's friend was at the distance of four or five miles from Damascus, situated
in a charming spot close to the Barrada, and in
an hour after our setting out, we found ourselves at
the gate. On entering the grounds, I was struck
with their extent and fertility, and could not
but admire the admirable order in which they
were kept. The fruit trees absolutely grew in
forests, and in every direction. The grounds were
intersected by rivulets, all of which were supplied
by the parent Barrada; while numerous camels,
of every age and breed, were seen here and there

cropping the well-watered pastures, or basking in the sun.

The interior of the house was, like the grounds by which it was surrounded, a model of wealth guided by a spirit of order. We found the table laid for dinner in a large saloon, in which were two marble fountains of very fine workmanship, deco-rated with a profusion of sweet-smelling flowers from the garden, the delicious odours from which were circulated throughout the vast chamber by the gentle currents of air, created by the constant sprinkling of water from the fountains.

Our party consisted of about forty persons. The large salver on which the viands are almost inva-riably served in the East was placed in the middle of the floor, which was covered with a rich Persian carpet, upon one of the most elegant stands I ever saw. It was made of cedar wood from Mount Lebanon, beautifully inlaid with mother-of-pearl, brought from the shores of the Red Sea. We seated ourselves in a circle around the salver, the men on one side and the women on the other; for, contrary to the practice prevailing at Mosul and Bagdad, the males and females of Christian families always dine together at the same table at

Damascus. Behind us stood a crowd of slaves with their hands crossed.

We had an excellent dinner. Besides roasts, pillaws, kababs, sambousack, and other dishes usually found at eastern tables, I tasted here a dish called "jild el faras," literally horses skin, which is a preparation of the Damascus apricots, so celebrated for their flavour and size, which are boiled in a mass, till they become a thick marmalade. This marmalade is reduced to a tolerable consistency, and then rolled out into a large sheet, a yard square, not thicker than the eighth part of an inch, which is then rolled like a wafer. The flavour is delicious. At this dinner, too, wine was served of various kinds; one of which, I remember, I found extremely agreeable. It was called Nebid el Asfar; it was of a gold colour, and I learned that the Italians import a considerable quantity of it.

It is the practice of the Greek Christians to enliven their meals with singing; hired musicians also attending with their instruments, which are, a sort of harp, flutes, and violins. Upon this occasion, every one was called on in his turn to take a share in the concert. Some sang religious songs, and others breathed forth soft, amorous, strains. At

last it came to my turn. Now I was no singer,
and my position was one of difficulty. I, however,
extricated myself from the dilemma, by prevailing
upon the daughter of the lady from Bassorah, who
had been my travelling companion from Bagdad,
to sing in my stead. She had a beautiful voice,
and the company consented to the substitution of
it for mine; by which assuredly they were great
gainers.

About four hours after dinner, which began at
one o'clock, we proceeded, as in Europe, to take
fruit, but in a separate chamber; after which
coffee and pipes, in the bowls of which aloe wood
was burnt, were served. This interval is allowed
to pass, from considerations of health; it being a
prevalent, and, I think, a correct opinion in these
countries, that fruit taken too soon after solid
food has a tendency to impair the digestion.

During dinner, a Turkish Aga, hot from a pilgrimage to Mecca, and resolved, after the custom
of travellers, to inflict on others, not only a
relation of the actual wonders which he had witnessed during his pious journey, but of some additional marvels which his imagination led him to
fancy he had seen, thought fit to single me out for

his victim upon this occasion. He had just come, he said, from paying a visit to the miraculous " Beyt Allah," or house of God, built by the hand of the Almighty himself. When the prophet paid a visit to the celestial regions, it is said that he saw this temple which, it seems, so took his fancy, that he was emboldened to ask it for the use of true believers here on earth. There was no resisting importunity coming from such a quarter, and accordingly the temple was sent down to Mecca, where it still exists, to the great consolation of all true Mussulmans, and utter confusion of all profane Kafirs, if any such unclean dogs should exist in the neighbourhood of the sanctuary; which, this devout Moslem assured me was guarded by angels, day and night. To the kaaba the true believer always turns his face in prayer; to the kaaba he every year, if his conscience should happen to be tender, sends presents; and to the kaaba he thinks himself bound, whatever his circumstances, at least once in his life, to make a pilgrimage, for the purpose of wiping out the stains of his iniquity, and making his face white before the holy prophet.

After Ramazan, three great caravans wend their way towards Mecca the Holy, from Bagdad, Da-

mascus, and Egypt, which seldom number fewer
than a hundred thousand pilgrims and two hundred thousand camels.   On their arrival at Mecca
they make the circuit of the mosque called Beyt
Ibrahim seven times.   They also think it " wajib,"
or necessary to their purification to kiss a remarkable black stone found at Mecca, which is said to
have descended from Heaven perfectly white, and
subsequently to have become black.

He then went on to relate to me the wonders of
the town of Koum, which contains the tomb of
Mahomet's daughter.   Three holy tombs, he told
me, are to be seen at Koum, the most magnificent
of which is that of Fatima, the daughter of the
prophet, and the wife of Ali, the star of the Shiah
sect, whose name is scarcely less sacred to the sons
of Irak, than that of Mahomet himself.   This
tomb he described as most magnificent; being
elevated to the height of about twelve feet, by
seven steps of massive silver, which go all round
it, and on which are spread the most costly stuffs,
embroidered with gold and studded with precious
stones.   Such, according to the Aga's account,
were the honour's paid to the divine Fatima, whom
true believers call the pure and immaculate virgin,

the chaste mother of the twelve illustrious vicars of Allah. The tomb did not, he assured me, hold the body of Fatima, who, he said, was lifted up to Heaven by the Almighty. The two other tombs at Koum he described as less splendid than that of the prophet's daughter, but still admirable, in point of structure and decoration.

I have frequently been not a little surprised to discover the veneration in which the name of our Blessed Lady and that of her Divine Son are held by the Turks and Persians. The loquacious Hadji, who favoured me with the above details, never mentioned these sacred names but in terms of respect, and yet I never met with a man more deeply imbued with the spirit of fanaticism, more completely the slave of credulity, or more strongly inspired with hatred for all Christians indiscriminately, of whatsoever denomination they might be.

We set out on our return to Damascus about sunset, and enjoyed a delightful ride along the bank of the Barrada, which was rendered doubly pleasant by the growing freshness of the coming twilight, and the westerly breeze which began to make its way from the sea over the icy summits of the Lebanon. It was nearly dark when we reached home, and we almost immediately after retired to rest, much pleased with our day's excursion.

The following morning, after breakfast, at about nine o'clock, I sallied forth, accompanied by my two travelling companions, to make purchases— in fact, to go shopping. We directed our steps towards the great bazaar, which adjoins the Khan Assad Pasha, and is so long that it takes half an hour to traverse it. Outside all was stillness; there was no sound of horse or carriage, nothing to indicate that the monotonous dead walls, which flanked the narrow streets on each side, contained a living soul; but once within, and your ears are stunned with a din of conversation, in languages as different as the costumes of the speakers.

Here was seen, mingling in the vast crowd, the portly Turk, the gaudy colours of whose dress offered a strong contrast to the homely garments of the Bedouin, enveloped in his coarse and ample aaba. Now and then an opulent Aga, splendidly clad in rich stuffs and furs, his girdle adorned with a jewel-hilted hanjar, and his sword trailing on the ground, was seen to pass along, with slow and stately pace, followed by ten or fifteen slaves, some of whom carried his nerghila and smoking apparatus, consisting of a capacious bag of cloth, so richly embroidered with gold, as almost to conceal the material of which it was composed, containing the tobacco and a pair of gold pincers wherewith to fill the pipe.

Besides these there were the manly and plainly-clad Druse and the Syrian Christian, whose dress at Damascus is far less sombre than that of the Christian of many other eastern cities; and, altogether, the effect produced upon our entering the bazaar was as picturesque and striking as can well be imagined, and far surpassed anything I had hitherto beheld of the kind.

We were conducted to the quarter where the Indian stuffs were sold, and I was astonished to behold the infinite variety and beautiful patterns of the silks shown to us by the dealers, whom I found the civilist of the civil. Indeed, the tradesmen of Damascus are noted for their courtesy and untiring assiduity. They will often assist a purchaser in finding an article which they themselves may not happen to have.

We bought several pieces of gold and silver tissue, of many shades and qualities, which are sold here at a very cheap rate; much lower than that at which I had been in the habit of purchasing them, and cheaper, as I afterwards discovered, than they can be procured any where in Palestine or the Lebanon.

As well as I can recollect, we paid about fifty shillings English for the quantity sufficient to make a ghombaz, or outer garment, together with the sleeves belonging to it, which are made very long and wide, reaching as low as the knee, when the arm is extended horizontally, and covering the hand. The quantity, I think, was fifteen draa, a measure equal to about three quarters of an English yard, and the width of the tissue was two feet. We also purchased a quantity of satin, of different tints, most of them of pure colours, and of a brilliancy such as I do not remember to have seen equalled in European manufacture, although the price was scarcely more than half that which I have paid for the latter article. The colours are so lasting that they retain their brilliancy when the fabric is worn to tatters; which also is a work of no little time, for the material is as thick as a board, and has a surface like glass. We bought five pieces of gold tissue, of all shades, at different shops, besides satins, stockings, embroidered slippers, and handkerchiefs, all of which were made up into a large packet, and entrusted to the care of a stout negro slave, who followed us.

Having completed our purchases, we strolled into the khan of Assad Pasha which adjoins the bazaar, professedly one of the finest khans in the world. I never remember to have seen so magnificent a cupola, except, perhaps, that of St. Peter's at Rome. From the khan we sallied forth to the banks of the stream, where we saw many groups smoking and drinking their coffee, in the numerous coffee-houses which peeped out at intervals amidst the shady groves of plane and other trees, which overhung the water and excluded the rays of the sun.

The inhabitants of Damascus are celebrated for their love of luxurious ease, as well as for their good countenances and graceful costume. Some of them, too, it would seem, are as much distinguished for their cunning as for their probity, if we may give credit to the proverb " Shami shumi,"—" The Damascenes are cunning." After wandering along the bank for a short time, we sat down to rest ourselves in the shade, and enjoy the prospect. Our attendant did the same; for the atmosphere began to grow warm, scarcely a breath of air was stirring, and his load was heavy. Having deposited it upon the bank of the canal, and placed himself by its side, whether he inadvertently tilted it or not, I cannot say, but our great horror may be easily imagined, when we beheld our morning's investment rolling down the bank with great velocity, and seeing it finally engulphed in the stream.

It was of no use to scold the poor fellow, who stood staring at the rapidly extending circles made by our sinking treasure, our dear, beautiful tissues, and our bewitching satins, with his mouth wide open, and his limbs trembling with apprehension. He was evidently more concerned than ourselves, and made every effort in his power to save his load. At length, while we were regarding each other with mutual consternation, a sudden thought seemed to flash across the negro's mind, for he started, smote his hard forehead with his clenched fist, and then darted off like a madman in the direction of the bazaar.

We knew not what to make of so extraordinary a proceeding. At first we thought that, fearing chastisement on reaching home, he had taken himself off altogether; but it was not long before

he set our doubts at rest, by returning in breathless haste, bringing with him a " rhathās," or professed diver, of which many are always loitering
about the bazaar, on the look out for employment.
The rhathās immediately plunged into the river,
and, after remaining long enough under the water
to have suffocated any ordinary human being,
returned to the surface empty handed. He again
and again descended, but still without success;
for the stream was rapid, and our packet had, no
doubt, been carried far away from the spot at
which it had rolled into the water. At last, our
patience being fairly exhausted, we returned home,
leaving the slave and the diver to continue their
search, without entertaining the smallest hope of
ever seeing our lost treasure again.

Next day, however, to our no small surprise, it
was brought to the house of Yusuf Hanhowri; but,
as may be easily imagined, in such a condition as
to be utterly valueless. Our Oriental resignation
to the will of God came happily to our aid, and
without giving way to useless regrets, we bore our
misfortune with all the fortitude of true Christians.

The house of Yusuf Hanhowri was very little
inferior in point of magnificence to those inhabited

by the Turks of the first distinction. It was uncommonly spacious; containing within its walls two distinct establishments; one for the males, and the other for the females. One of the saloons was, I remember, remarkably splendid. The ceiling was covered with beautiful arabesque and gilding. On the wall, just below the ceiling, was a row of small apertures, for the purpose of admiting air and light, closed by gratings carved into a graceful and fanciful design, and gilt. In the middle of the room were two fountains, and its sides were occupied by an aviary, containing parrots, nightingales, and birds of every description, of beautiful plumage and delightful song. It is not uncommon to see strange doves fly into the apartment, and, after refreshing themselves at the fountain, quietly take their departure. It is said, I know not with what truth, that this habit is not unfrequently turned to account by amorous swains and love-sick damsels, who convert this bird, the emblem of pure affection, into a clandestine letter-carrier,—the bearer of their tender correspondence.

The floor was spread with the most costly carpets from Persia. At the end of the room was a dais, raised about one foot from the floor, covered with the finest carpet, on which the host habitually received his most distinguished guests. The walls were covered with the most varied Arabesque designs, enriched with gilding. In the midst of such splendour as this, it is not un-common to see a child's cradle placed on a piece of plain board, which is laid upon the carpet, and rocked by the mother; who, together with her female relations, is usually occupied in ornamental needle-work and embroidery, in which they are great adepts. I have seen napkins and handker-chiefs, on which they had executed their skill, which were splendid specimens of this art. It is looked upon as little short of a crime, save where the illness of the mother renders such a step a duty of humanity, for a female to refuse suckling her own child; in which respect they resemble the Nomadic tribes, amongst which a similar feel-ing prevails. The conversation of the Christian women, with whom I associated at Damascus, was marked by good sense, and indicated great purity of thought; and the greatest care is used to keep from the minds of girls anything which might

have a tendency to corrupt them, or to instil ideas
unsuitable to their age and condition.

In the presence of strangers, the customs of
Christian families are as rigid as those of the
Turks. Husband and wife are not to be distinguished from total strangers by their deportment;
a salute, or even touch of the hand, being regarded,
on such occasions, as a very great breach of
decorum. Amongst the women, the Saturday is
entirely devoted to the bath, and the Friday to
the making the necessary preparations for the
enjoyment of that luxury. I observed that the
strictest attention was paid, by the Christian ladies
of Damascus, to their religious duties; and I have
often known them to forego both breakfast and
dinner, rather than neglect mass, or vespers.

The master of the house spends the greater part
of the day in his own separate apartments, in the
enjoyment of his pipe, which is seldom out of his
mouth; while a fingan of coffee is brought by an
attendant every quarter of an hour. Great display
is made, and a considerable sum of money lavished
on the decoration of their pipes. I saw some at
the house of Yusuf Hanhowri, which were exceed-

ingly splendid in their mounting, and must have cost him a little fortune. Many of the amber mouth-pieces were mounted with gold and precious stones. Besides the pipe, the men, both Turks and Christians, occupy themselves with rosaries of large amber beads, which they let fall one after another, reciting prayers.

CHAPTER XI.

A visit to the Aga's Lady—Noble Prospect—Christian Aspirations—A perilous Project —Good Advice —Visit to a Mosque—A Dilemma—A Panic—A Catastrophe—An agreeable Surprise.

Not a day passed in which I did not receive a message from the Aga's wife by one of her slaves, urging me to redeem my promise to pay her an early visit; so that I was compelled at last to go, although not desiring the interview. This time I went entirely alone; and upon reaching the Aga's abode, I was forthwith ushered into the saloon appropriated to the female part of the establishment, where I found my fair friend, together with many beautiful Georgians, busily engaged in embroidering and making silk shirts, of beautiful texture, and ornamented with lace, for their lord; as well as the muslin which encircles the tarbaush, which they also ornament with lace. Their work showed extraordinary skill and dexterity, and was evidently the result of long and almost undivided devotion to the needle; for, except on bathing days, they were seldom permitted to stir abroad, and when they did, they were always taken out of the city by slaves, in the tahterawan, or sedan chair, which is surrounded by curtains, in order to exclude the unholy gaze of the stranger; which, according to the Moslem notions, is, of itself, sufficient to pollute.

The effect of these restraints, and the fuss which an airing unavoidably produces, considerably allay the desire to seek diversion and exercise in the open air, away from the grounds of the husband, and circumscribe the enjoyment derived from it: added to which, they could none of them, with, perhaps, the single exception of my friend, either read or write; having, in the majority of cases, been purchased very young; so that their needle was almost their only resource. Young as they were, however, when forced within the pale of Islam, many of these Georgians, Christians by birth, still cherished a longing to return to the faith of their fathers, and showed me, an open professor of Christianity, more respect than they would have paid to the Sultan himself. On learning that I was about to proceed straight from Damascus to El Khods el Sherifa, Jerusalem the Noble, they exclaimed, one and all, " Haniāh leki ya Hajiah jenabhi saīdah ; " — " A blessing attend thee, oh pilgrim! what happiness is thine !" " Ezkerīna fi daaki ;"—" Remember us in thy prayers."

Having gone through the usual ceremony of washing in the lackan, coffee, sherbet, nerghilahs, and perfumes, were served, and we remained engaged in conversation till dinner time, which was fixed between mid-day and one o'clock. The repast was worthy of the wealthy Aga out of whose coffers it was provided, and the attendants were more numerous, I think, than I had ever before seen on similar occasions; in fact, they seemed to be almost in each other's way.

I rose to take leave shortly after dinner, but my enthusiastic friend would not hear of my quitting her so soon. A messenger was therefore despatched to the house of my host, to acquaint my friends that I purposed remaining the night at the Aga's

house. In the afternoon, we went on the magnificent terrace at the top of the house, to enjoy the
evening breeze. The view was superb beyond all
description; for at the elevation at which we were,
—besides the forest of fruit trees, extending for
thirty miles round the city, undulating in the
breeze, like the waves of the sea; besides the
tapering minarets, whose polished tiles shone with
a deep glow, like burnished gold; besides the graceful cupolas and majestic domes which surrounded
us on every side; besides the hoary Anti-Lebanon,
towering in the distance, its furrowed sides fast
filling with a sea of deepening purple;—the generous
Barrada pouring forth, without stint, its treasures
on every side, to fertilize and adorn the noble
city, was plainly to be descerned wending its
way.

Long after the rest of the Aga's ladies had
quitted the terrace I remained lost in rapture,
with my eyes fixed on the charming scene around
me, with no other companion but my engaging
friend. A message was sent up to say that the
dessert was spread below; but I entreated my
companion that we should remain where we were,
as long as the light lasted; to which she readily

consented, and ordered our fruit to be spread on the terrace.

As the shades of evening approached, our thoughts took a pious turn, and our conversation was naturally on religious subjects. " What joys," I exclaimed, "may not the true Christian hope for, when, at the termination of his earthly career, it shall please the Almighty to call him to the enjoyment of eternal happiness in the realms of bliss, if it be given to us mortals to behold such a scene as this now before us! Let us, then, learn to raise our thoughts from these beautiful works to their all-bountiful Creator, who has still greater blessings in store for us."

The Aga's wife burst into tears. " How shall my tongue utter these things," she said, wringing her hands, " for I am an outcast, and have no inheritance in Heaven? My birthright is gone ; my soul is in bondage."

" Be comforted!" I exclaimed; "who can say what trials the Almighty Father may decree that his children should endure, to try their faith? Do not give way to despair: put your trust in God, and He will not fail you in the hour of need."

Without making any reply, she threw herself

on her knees, and passionately clasping her hands,
lifted her beautiful eyes, glistening with tears and
glowing with ardent supplication, to Heaven, exclaimed, " Remove from my neck, O merciful
Father! the yoke of the infidel, for my burden
presses sore, and I have no strength to help me.
Take me once more unto thy holy communion,
lest I perish in my sin!" The outburst of long
pent up remorse evidently afforded relief to my
sorrowing friend; who soon sufficiently recovered
her serenity to venture down—for it was now
growing dark—into the saloon below.

On reaching it, we found the ladies assembled,
and not a little surprised at our long stay on the
terrace. Shortly after the Aga entered, accompanied by his father; whereupon the ladies, one
and all, immediately put on the turha, or veil,
which conceals the entire face, with the exception
of the eyes. Games were now introduced, to
while away the time. One of these was that called
" fanagin," in which several cups or " fingans,"
and a ring, are used. The ring is concealed under
one of the cups, and one of the company is set to
work, blindfolded, to find it, under a penalty
which is settled by the company. Chess was also

introduced. Thus, what with talking, and playing at different games, we managed to pass the evening pleasantly enough, and even my sad friend seemed to have, in some degree, recovered her spirits.

At eleven o'clock, I was shown to the apartment prepared for me, which was situated in a remote corner of the harem. I slept soundly, and rose early on the following morning, remaining, according to my invariable custom, for some time occupied in my devotions, which the secluded situation of my apartment enabled me to perform without fear of interruption.

No sooner had the Aga gone out than my enthusiastic friend contrived to slip away from her companions, and join me in my chamber. She came with a firmly settled determination to concert measures with me for her escape from the thraldom of Islam. The almost insurmountable dangers which intervened between her and her desperate purpose, and the awful punishment which must fall on her devoted head, in the event of detection, were alike unheeded. She had taken the probability of a cruel death into her calculations, and had made up her mind to the worst.

She knew that I was about to set out shortly for

the Lebanon, and the object of her present visit to me was to induce me to take her with me. Her request startled me. I well knew the dreadful penalty which she as well as myself must inevitably incur, in case of discovery; and, although I might have disregarded it as far as I was personally concerned, having for many years contemplated the possibility of suffering martyrdom in the cause of the true faith, I nevertheless could not view without a shudder, the prospect of delivering up so fair a creature to so cruel a death.

" Think of the dangers which beset you on every side," I exclaimed.

" I have, I have," was her answer; " but what are they, that they should bar my passage on the road to the mansions of the true God?"

" The Aga is powerful," I exclaimed; " his slaves are told by hundreds; he speaks the word, and his horsemen cover the desert. Are we foxes, that we should escape his vigilance? Here you have riches and plenty; your wishes are laws; the Aga is himself your slave. Think, then, once more, before you exchange all these enjoyments for penury, stripes, and an ignominious death."

" I know," she replied, " that the Aga is power-

ful. I know that certain death will be my lot, if
my evil destiny should frustrate my attempt to
escape. All this I have pondered over and over
again in my mind; but neither poverty, nor
stripes, nor the dread of death itself have power
to change my resolution. If it be the will of God
that I should perish in the glorious attempt, I am
ready to bid adieu to life, in the cause of His holy
faith. You, who have always exhorted me to be
stedfast and hold fast to the Rock of Salvation,
how is it that you would now recommend to me to
look to riches and honours, rather than to turn my
thoughts to Heaven, and renounce all for the
love of God?"

True, I had many times and often so exhorted
her, and my pupil was now in her turn become my
instructress. I felt quite ashamed of the truckling,
time-serving counsels which my anxiety for her
personal safety had but just now prompted me to
offer. My fears, however, soon vanished; I became
as enthusiastic as herself. I determined to unite
my fate with her's, for good or for ill. I entered
at once warmly and heartily into her scheme. I
fell upon her neck, and we shed warm tears of
joy, not unmingled with fear and sad forebodings.

We proceeded together to the saloon in which
the Aga's wife was in the habit of passing the
greater part of her time. Finding, fortunately, no
one there, we had leisure to form our plans, and arrange the scheme of our future operations. Amongst
the various pipes and nerghilahs which adorn the
walls of this saloon, all more or less costly in their
fittings up, was one of superb workmanship and
rare materials, which the Aga had lately presented
to his favourite, as a gift worthy the acceptance of
one whom he professed to love with so much tenderness. The mouth was of silver gilt, inlaid with
precious stones of considerable value. This she
pressed me much to accept, as a proof of her
unalterable esteem. Knowing the considerations
under which it had been presented to her, I was
extremely loth to take advantage of her kindness ;
but the more I persisted in declining the proffered gift, the more pressing and determined she
appeared to grow in her entreaties.

While we were thus warmly engaged in this
friendly contest, who should enter but the Aga
himself. On learning the cause of our dispute,
he, somewhat to my surprise, I confess, lent his
entreaties to hers, that I would accept the present

which she was so anxious to force upon me. It was sufficient that she willed it: had the gift been ten times more valuable, he would have insisted on my taking it. After such urgent entreaties from a dear friend, seconded by those of the man with whose wealth the bauble had been purchased, I must have been a very stock or a stone to have refused a nerghila, on whose exquisite beauties even Hafiz or Ferdousi would not have disdained to lavish his sweetest flowers of poetry. I accepted it.

After some conversation on indifferent matters, the Aga took his departure, and it was not long before I followed his example; not, however, before I had given his wife a pledge that I would be incessant in my endeavours to carry into effect the object dearest to her heart. Accordingly, upon reaching home, I sought the good bishop, who had been my travelling companion from Bagdad, in order to consult him as to the best mode of proceeding in so delicate a matter; not in the least doubting that his age and experience would be able to suggest a better plan than the one which our own rash and untutored intellects could hope to discover, and fully expecting to find in him a zealous and eager coadjutor in so pious an undertaking.

Imagine, then, my grief and surprise—I had almost said my indignation—when I found the worthy man cold to indifference! He magnified the danger to be apprehended, and appeared, to my perhaps over enthusiastic mind, greatly to underrate the vast importance of the object in view. Although grieved and mortified beyond conception at this unexpected apathy, on the part of one on whom I had so confidently reckoned for sage counsel and prompt assistance in the furtherance of my object, I, nevertheless, did not yield myself up to despair, but determined to redeem, if possible, the pledge I had given to my unhappy friend, alone and unassisted, save by Him who is ever at hand to aid the friendless.

Scarcely a day passed on which I did not spend a portion of it with my new friend. We visited the Pasha's zenana together. The arrangements of the courts and apartments did not differ in any material degree from those of the zenanas of other great and opulent Turks; save that the rooms were more vast and more splendid in their decorations than any I had yet beheld. Silks, velvets, and gold embroidery were seen on every side, until the eye almost wearied with the contemplation of so much wealth and magnificence. The musnuds were the richest I ever saw, covered with velvet and embroidery. The gardens were, I think, half as large as the Regent's Park, and nothing was wanting to make the inmates the happiest of mortals, save liberty, mental culture, and that peace of mind which power and wealth cannot purchase. In nearly every apartment of the harem, turtle doves sent forth their melancholy notes, lulling the mind into a pleasing sadness: neither was there any lack of many-hued parrots to dissipate melancholy, and enliven the fair occupants with their amusing loquaciousness.

One day, the Aga's wife solicited me to accompany her to the great mosque. This was a serious matter; for should an unbeliever be found polluting the sacred precincts with his unhallowed presence, his audacity would, I knew, be punished with instant death. My friend was, it is true, the wife of one of the most influential men in Damascus; but this would have availed nothing in the event of detection. She, however, was bent upon my going. She assured me she could so effectually disguise me, that it would be quite impossible for the most zealous and lynx-eyed Moslem to detect the imposition. Her assurances quieted my scruples, as I was not a little anxious to witness their religious ceremonies. We accordingly set out one Friday morning on an expedition which, haply, might have cost me my head. From top to toe, I was dressed completely *à la Turque*, and we were both closely veiled, preceded and followed by six slaves. We were not long in gaining the mosque, the Aga's house being hard by the straight street in which it is situated.

We entered the awful precincts—doubly awful to a Christian at Damascus, on account of the headlong fanaticism which prevails in this grand resort of pious and not unthrifty hadjis. We ascended the gallery — the place set apart for women—where we found several already assembled. The congregation below having seated themselves on the marble pavement, which was spread with the finest Persian carpets, the Mollah ascended his pulpit, which was situated in the midst of them, and began his exhortation, which

lasted about half an hour, and was sufficiently
entertaining.

He began with expounding, and concluded with
exhortation. I was very much amused with the
manner in which he accounted for the Mussulman
prohibition against eating pork. " When Noe
took into the ark the male and female of every
creature living on the earth, he said, ' the pig was
not created, but was engendered afterwards by the
vast mass of ordure accumulated by the elephant.'"
In another part of his sermon, adverting to the
failure of Mahomet when, in imitation of Moses,
he struck the bare rock in the presence of a multitude of his disciples, expecting water to leap forth
at his command, he said, that the disaster was not
caused by any want of supernatural power in the
holy prophet, or by any disinclination on the part
of the water to obey his inspired injunction, but
because the well had been undermined by pigs,
who had so turned up the ground by means of
their snout and paws, that the water had entirely
escaped, and there was none left to come forth.

My friend told me that this same learned ex-
pounder thus described, upon a former occasion,
the mode in which the faithful, after a life spent in

deeds of virtue and holiness, will be finally transported to the realms of bliss. " The prophet," he said, " will come in the form of a lamb, in whose ample fleece the host of true believers will, in the form of vermin, congregate; so that, when the sacred animal shall be called on high, the elect will be shaken out into endless happiness."

The doctrinal part being disposed of, the preacher next entered upon a glowing exhortation to the cultivation of the true faith, and its propagation, without scruple as to the means employed, sparing neither fire nor sword, persecutions nor exactions, chains nor slavery, for the accomplishment of this hallowed end.

Having thus thoroughly awakened his audience to the necessity of following in the footsteps of the founder of their faith, the mollah descended from his pulpit, and, standing in the midst, called on all present to join in prayer. Whereupon the men below immediately arose from the carpet, and stood around their priest, in an attitude of reverence. " La hāoul wala kouat ila b' Allah,"—there is neither aid nor strength save in God,—cried the mollah, in a loud voice; " God created us, and to him we shall return." These words were repeated by the congregation, accompanied with many reverential salams and turnings of heads, first to the right and then to the left; and so the mollah proceeded to read many other passages from the Koran, the people repeating as before, and varying their attitudes according to the import of the prayer, bowing the head, sitting on their heels (an attitude of reverence amongst the Mahomedans), and prostrating themselves at the name of Allah and the prophet. The women, in the gallery, also took part in the ceremony, remaining almost as closely veiled as when they were walking in the public streets.

So far all had proceeded well enough. I had had full leisure to observe the ceremony, and my disguise seemed to have effectually screened me from discovery. The service being concluded, we were about to depart, and were arranging our veils for this purpose, when I observed that the eyes of one or two of the ladies in the gallery were intently fixed upon my face. I felt alarmed, and pressed my companion to hasten our departure. In the meantime there was much whispering amongst our sister devotees, accompanied at intervals with furtive glances and scowling looks towards me. I had

evidently become an object of general interest.
The sounds soon changed from anxious whispering
to loud and angry murmurs. " Ghiaour fi'l jamaa—
an infidel pollutes the sanctuary," cried one; " I
know her features well; for did I not see her at
the bath?" " Ente wraltana—you are mistaken,"
cried another, " it is impossible." " Wadhaiāt el
nebbi ena maakeda—by the life of the prophet I
am certain !" replied the first.

Alarmed at these hostile comments, which were
uttered loud enough to reach my ear, I besought
my companion to delay no longer. " Fear nothing,"
said she, " on my head be your safety. Let us see
who will dare to offend the friend of the Aga's wife."
Thus encouraged, I followed her to the door of the
mosque, with a steady and fearless pace, carefully
avoiding all appearance of anxiety, or trepidation.
Once outside the sanctuary, we made all speed
towards the Aga's house, which we reached in a
shorter time than we had taken in going to the
mosque a few hours before. Short, however, as it
was, every moment was to me one of terror and
alarm; nor did I think myself in safety, until I was
fairly housed within the palace.

We now began to deliberate as to what course it

would be best for me to take, under such critical circumstances; for it was clear that I, a Christian, had been discovered in the act of polluting with my presence those holy precincts, from which the law of the Turkish empire rigorously excludes all but true Moslems, under pain of death. I could not doubt but that those who had detected my disguise would, in their desire to do acceptable service to the prophet and his followers, take the earliest opportunity of denouncing me to the authorities. My only chance of preservation lay, therefore, in concealment.

To have returned to the house of my host, himself a Christian, and consequently an object of dislike and abhorrence, besides being more than half suspected of being very wealthy, would have been to put my head, as it were, into the lion's mouth, besides incurring the risk of involving my generous host in my own embarrassments, in which he had had no concern whatever, and consigning him, together with his amiable family, to ruthless oppression, and perhaps utter destruction. Yielding, therefore, to entreaties, I agreed to remain, for some days at least, under the Aga's roof, there to await the issue of my unfortunate adventure.

Day after day passed over my head without any visit from the officers of justice, although every sound of a fresh arrival threw both my anxious friend and myself into a state of alarm, lest it should prove to be the khadi. For my own part, I entertained but faint hopes of ultimately escaping detection in such a place as Damascus, where nearly the entire Mussulman population are inflamed by an intolerant bigotry. I therefore endeavoured to resign myself to the idea of martyrdom.

In this painful state of suspense, scarcely less dreadful than the certainty of speedy punishment, I one day heard an unusual stir in the house, as though a person of importance had just honoured us with a visit. I was breathless with expectation, but nevertheless dared not to emerge from my place of concealment. I was, however, not kept long in suspense; for in the course of a very few minutes my friend rushed into the room with terror painted on her countenance, which was pale as death.

" Haste ! haste !" she cried, "and conceal yourself in the most secluded part of the harem. The khadi is come—I have myself seen him. Lose not an instant! I will do everything in my power to baffle their search." I thereupon quitted the room in great trepidation, and sped me as fast as my feet would carry me, to a lumber room in a remote and unfrequented part of the harem.

The question now was as to the best mode of concealment. Casting my eyes around me, I espied in a corner a large roll of Indian matting, which had been recently removed from one of the lower rooms by the negresses, in order that they might clean the floor. I immediately went upon my knees, and crept cautiously into this huge rouleau, and there awaited the issue, with all the patience and resignation I could muster; conscious that I had taken every precaution in my power to preserve my life. For the space of at least half an hour all was still as death. Not a sound could I hear of what was passing in the house. The flurry and excitement into which my friend's announcement had temporarily thrown me had subsided, and was succeeded by a complete calm, I might almost say serenity of mind; and had it not been for the inconvenient and confined situation in which I was placed, I could have abandoned myself to a pleasing reverie.

" But, hark! I hear a sound in the distance! They are searching the rooms below," thought I. My incipient reverie was instantly at an end, and my heart again began to beat with anxiety. It was plainly the noise of footsteps, and not of one, but of several individuals. It became louder and more distinct at every instant. Now I heard them on the landing, immediately below the room in which I lay concealed. " Alas! alas!" I cried, " my dear, kind-hearted friend, your efforts, then, have been all in vain! I am discovered, and we shall both pay the penalty of our rashness."

They were now at the very door! Big drops stood upon my forehead. I was nearly choked with the effort to suppress the sound of my breathing. As far as I could judge from the noise, there appeared to be only two persons; but as yet I could see nothing of them. They approached the roll of matting in which I lay concealed. I was on the point of surrendering myself, when I bethought myself of reconnoitring the enemy through a hole in the matting.

I leave the reader to conceive what my joy must have been when, instead of the "jind," or officers of justice, I found these much-dreaded personages to be no other than about ten negresses of the establishment, who had brought up some additional lumber. I was delighted, and was inwardly returning thanks to Providence for my preservation thus far, when I felt a heavy load thrown on the top of the roll of matting in which I lay, which almost made me scream, from the suddenness of the shock. After this came another and then another, until I was almost compelled to cry aloud for mercy, and was fairly buried alive.

Feeling that it was now become a serious matter, indeed a question of life or death, I made one desperate effort to extricate myself; in doing which I gave the roll of matting an impulse forwards, so sudden and violent, that the negresses set up a scream of terror, and rushed out of the room, crying aloud, "a geni! a geni!" leaving me to my own ingenuity to extricate myself as I best might. It was undoubtedly an amusing scene, and one which I should myself have greatly enjoyed, had I not been in imminent danger of suffocation.

I made several ineffectual struggles to disengage myself, but without success, and was beginning to think that the labours of the negresses would have rendered the proceedings of the khadi superfluous, when I heard the light cheerful step of the Aga's wife, familiar to my ear, tripping up the stairs. She hastily entered the room, and, after looking around her, called me by my name. I could, however, with difficulty make myself heard, owing to the thickness of the matting, and the state of approaching suffocation at which I had arrived.

At length she heard my voice, and, by a great effort, succeeded after some time in removing the mass of matting by which I was covered, and I emerged at last, such a picture of disorder as no mortal ever before beheld; my hair all about my face, and my countenance begrimed with dirt. I rushed into my friend's arms, and she told me it was indeed the khadi who had come, but his visit was on official business with the Aga, and I had incurred the risk of suffocation without cause. Our mutual congratulations over, we both began to perceive the ludicrous side of the picture, and descended to her room, laughing till the tears ran down our cheeks.

Day after day passed without any fresh alarm, and I at length resolved to return to my friends, to make arrangements for our speedy departure for

the Lebanon, in the full confidence that my imprudent freak had not come to the knowledge of the
authorities; not, however, before I had fully ma-
tured the plan by which my warm-hearted friend
was to be delivered from her thraldom. Having
described to her my proposed route, and furnished
her with the name of the convent where she was
to join me, I embraced her affectionately and took
my departure.

END OF VOL. I.

PRINTED BY WILLIAM WILCOCKSON, ROLLS BUILDINGS, FETTER LANE.

Made in the USA
San Bernardino, CA
02 June 2014